Is Lighter Better?

Is Lighter Better?

Skin-Tone Discrimination among Asian Americans

Joanne L. Rondilla
and
Paul Spickard

Contributing Researchers and Writers
Lilynda Agvateesiri
Monica Chum
Sara Cruz
Luz Devadason
Holly Hoegi
Karen Jackson
Lynn Kawabe
Christie Trieu
Charmaine Tuason
Mey Year

ROWMAN & LITTLEFIELD PUBLISHERS, INC.
Lanham • Boulder • New York • Toronto • Plymouth, UK

ROWMAN & LITTLEFIELD PUBLISHERS, INC.

Published in the United States of America
by Rowman & Littlefield Publishers, Inc.
A wholly owned subsidiary of The Rowman & Littlefield Publishing Group, Inc.
4501 Forbes Boulevard, Suite 200, Lanham, Maryland 20706
www.rowmanlittlefield.com

Estover Road, Plymouth PL6 7PY, United Kingdom

British Library Cataloguing in Publication Information Available

Library of Congress Cataloging-in-Publication Data

Rondilla, Joanne L.
  Is lighter better? : skin-tone discrimination among Asian Americans / Joanne L. Rondilla
and Paul Spickard.
    p. cm.
  Includes bibliographical references and index.
  ISBN-13: 978-0-7425-5493-1 (cloth : alk. paper)
  ISBN-10: 0-7425-5493-7 (cloth : alk. paper)
  ISBN-13: 978-0-7425-5494-8 (paper : alk. paper)
  ISBN-10: 0-7425-5494-5 (paper : alk. paper)
  1. Asian Americans—Race identity. 2. Asian Americans—Attitudes. 3. Race dis-
crimination—United States. 4. Racism—United States. 5. Human skin color—United
States—Psychological aspects. 6. Human skin color—Social aspects—United States.
7. United States—Race relations. 8. Asian Americans—Social conditions. I. Spickard,
Paul R., 1950- II. Title.
  E184.A75R66 2007
  305.895'073--dc22

                                                                    2006028999

Printed in the United States of America

⊗™ The paper used in this publication meets the minimum requirements of American
National Standard for Information Sciences—Permanence of Paper for Printed Library
Materials, ANSI/NISO Z39.48-1992.

To our darker and lighter sisters and brothers

Contents

Acknowledgments

This book is the product of a team of scholars, each of whom contributed her or his part, and each of whom is grateful for the insights shared by the others in the course of the study. We are also indebted to our colleagues in Asian American Studies 137 at UC Santa Barbara (UCSB), who in class discussions brought up many of the issues that led us into this study.

Earlier versions of chapters 3 and 4 were presented to the Association for Asian American Studies, the Ethnic Studies Department of the University of California, Berkeley, the Center for the Humanities at Oregon State University, and the Multi-Cultural Center at UCSB. We are grateful for the support of those institutions and the comments and suggestions we received from several listeners in those places.

Ambi Harsha, Jane Iwamura, Chrissy Lau, and Lori Pierce shared marketing materials and insights on the selling of skin lighteners. Among those who provided ideas and bibliographical suggestions were Neil Davison, Rudy Guevarra, Luke Roberts, and Chikako Shinagawa. Margaret Hunter generously allowed us to read an advance manuscript copy of her book on Black women and Mexican American and colorism. Mai Trieu helped with data gathering, analysis, and translation. Ashwini Ashokumar, Gina Oh, Helen Lee, and Akshata Mankikar helped with the research. Luz Devadason, Joy Ipac, Chrissy Lau, Robin Le, Marybeth Liu, Yenyy Sihapanya, and Sunny Yang consented to have their writing included in chapters 1 and 2. Countless Asian American friends told us we were on the right track as we pursued this investigation. Grace Ebron at AltaMira Press was a model editor, followed ably by Jessica Gribble at Rowman & Littlefield. We are grateful to them all.

In addition, Joanne Rondilla would like to congratulate the people who contributed their time and insights to this project. Your hard work and belief in this project is what kept us going. A big and long overdue thank you to Vicente Diaz, whose support throughout the years (even before I was a graduate student) has been immeasurable. I would also like to thank my committee members Catherine Ceniza Choy, Paul Spickard, Magaret Hunte, Michael Omi, and Marcial Gonzales for their time, wisdom, and encouragement. Patricia Penn Hilden has also been an incredible inspiration since the moment I stepped on to the Berkeley campus. I thank you for your strength and honesty in this grueling process. Parts of this project were developed during various seminars I took. The following scholars deserve my gratitude for allowing me the space to work through these ideas: Ronald Takaki, Evelyn Nakano-Glenn, and Ramon Grosfoguel. Fortunately, I have been surrounded by wonderful colleagues whose belief in my work and life's endeavors has meant the world to me. *Maraming salamat* to the Critical Filipina/Filipino Studies Collective (CFFSC): Gladys Nubla, Peter Chua, Lucy Burns, Robyn Rodriguez, Rowena Tomaneng, Nerissa Balce, Jeffrey Santa Ana, and Richard Chu for showing me that a commitment to scholarship and to our communities are not mutually exclusive. To the Indigenous Pacific Islander Alliance (IPIA) of UC Berkeley: David "Vika" Palaita and Mikey Tuncap, thank you so much for your spirit and laughter. To the American Indian Graduate Student Association (AIGSA) of UC Berkeley (Majel Boxer, Danika Medak-Saltzman, and Dory Nason), your dedication, strength, and commitment inspire me. To the Critical Filipina/Filipino Studies Working Group of UC Berkeley, may the work we do continue. Finally, I would like to thank my mother, Sonia L. Rondilla, my brother, Gerry Rondilla, and my sister, Cristina Tydingco, and her family (Norbert, Sonia Ann, Theoren, and Brendan) for their love and patience as I go through the motions of academia. This process would be so much harder if I did not have you there to guide me.

• / •

Colorism in Asian America

*N*arrow streams run silently down the young woman's cheeks. Her perfect makeup is slowly dissolving. She pays no heed to the tears, nor to the puddled stains that grow on her blouse. Quietly she talks about her pain. She is beautiful and does not feel it. Sparkling black eyes sit in almond folds above a button nose. Ebony hair cascades down her back. Her tawny skin is smooth, lustrous, and blemish-free. Her waist is thin, her limbs cleanly formed.

And she wants to change it all. In her purse she carries blue contact lenses and a tube of skin bleach. She has an appointment this afternoon with a hairdresser to lighten and streak. Tomorrow she is scheduled to consult a surgeon about new eyes, a new nose, and a new bust. "I'm just so tired of being ugly," she says.

This woman's dilemma is not unique. Millions of women, of all ages and countries and ethnicities, feel pressure to look different than they do, to gain the esteem of others and acceptance in their own eyes. Some men feel similar pressures, though not so often and seldom with as much force; for in nearly all human societies beauty is more rigorously required of women than of men. Men can feel good about themselves on the basis of power, wealth, and achievement. Women in industrial societies gain self-esteem from those things, too, but they are also required to be beautiful or at least to present themselves beautifully. And beauty is judged by fairly common standards: symmetrical features, large eyes, smooth skin, silky hair, a slim waist. Thus, the fashion and cosmetic industries are among the biggest of international businesses—and they direct the vast bulk of their attention to women.

For women who are not White,[1] much of the beauty issue is concentrated around the color and texture of their skin. The prime value is placed on being light and smooth, and such qualities can affect one's life chances significantly. This is colorism. Cedric Herring, a sociologist of the phenomenon,

1

defines colorism as "discriminatory treatment of individuals falling within the same 'racial' group on the basis of skin color." That is, some people, particularly women, are treated better or worse on account of the color of their skin relative to other people who share their same racial category. Herring notes that, while skin color is the master marker of such difference, other physical attributes, such as hair and eye color, hair texture, and nose and eye shape, also contribute to such distinctions and discriminations. These discriminations are made by members of the dominant White group as they view people of color, and they are also made within communities of color.[2]

ASIAN AMERICANS AND COLORISM

The weeping woman described at the beginning of this chapter is an Asian American, the daughter of Vietnamese immigrants. Her desire is to have lighter skin and hair, rounder eyes, a higher bridge to her nose, and a larger bustline. Some would say that she wanted to look like a White woman, and they would likely criticize her for it. Others would say that her desires for lightness and different features and body shape had origins in Asia, where they were products of Asian class imperatives not a move toward Whiteness.

Whether she wanted to look White or had some other ambition, this woman is not alone. Rare indeed is the Asian American who has not heard an aunt or grandmother say something like: "Don't go out in the sun. You'll get too dark." The worship of tanned bodies is a Euro-American fetish, not one honored by Asian American families and communities. In the film *Mississippi Masala*, twenty-five-year-old Meena's mother is eager to find a husband for her daughter and sets her sights on Harry Patel. Meena, wanting to stretch her wings beyond rural Mississippi and is not so interested in being set up, says to her mother, "Face it, Ma. You've got a darkie daughter. Harry's mother doesn't like darkies." A female wedding guest comments disparagingly on Meena's chances: "You can be dark and have money, or you can be fair and have no money. But you can't be dark and have no money and get Harry Patel." Charmaine Tuason, a Filipina in her early twenties and one of the interviewers for this study, wrote of her own experience: "'Your daughter is a dark beauty,' said an aunt to my mother. Instead of being flattered I was quite put off by her statement. When someone in the Filipino community calls you dark, they don't mean beauty at all."[3]

In every Asian American community, colorism is a widely recognized but largely unremarked-on consensus. That is, people understand that there are some kinds of skin color, hair and eye color, shape of eyes and noses, and so forth that are viewed as preferable to others. This is particularly true among young people in the dating, mating, and marriage mart. It is truer for women than for men. But it seems to be true in substantial degree for Asian Americans of many ages and both sexes.

Is Lighter Better? attempts to explain this phenomenon. What are the colorism issues that operate in Asian American communities? Are they the same issues for all sorts of Asian Americans—for women and for men, for immigrants and the American born, for Chinese, Filipinos, Koreans, Vietnamese, and all the other sorts of Asian Americans? Do they reflect a desire to look like White people, or is some other motive at work?

Some of the colorism issues seem to have been carried over from Asia. One cannot travel long in Thailand and not be struck by the ubiquity of skin lightening lotions in markets and drug stores. In almost every country in Asia, the celebrity class, and especially movie stars, are noticeably lighter and taller, with more angular features, than the general population. V. S. Naipaul wrote about caste and colorism in India in his novel *Half a Life*. When protagonist Willie Chandron's father decided to rebel against his Brahmin family, the most extreme form of protest he could make was to marry a dark-skinned woman of lower caste:

> My decision was to . . . marry the lowest person I could find. . . . There was a girl at the university. I didn't know her. I hadn't spoken to her. I had merely noticed her. She was small and coarse-featured, almost tribal in appearance, noticeably black. . . . [I wanted to marry] the blackness of her skin. She would have belonged to a backward caste. . . . I was fascinated and repelled by her. She would have been of the very low. It would have been unbearable to consider her family and clan and their occupations. When people like that went to the temple they would have been kept out of the sanctum, the inner cell with the image of the deity. The officiating priest would never have wanted to touch those people.[4]

His bride's low caste and dark skin were associated in his mind with coarse features, poverty, lack of education, primitiveness, uncleanness, even ritual impurity. Willie's grandfather "went wild. All his tolerance and kindness disappeared. He became heart-broken. . . . He said at last, 'You've blackened all our faces. . . . Now you've thrown our inheritance away.'" Willie's father and his family associated Willie's mother's dark skin, and the dark skin she passed on to her children, with "shame," a "taint," "slyness," and "polluting."[5]

Not every Asian country has had social hierarchies that have carried the intensity of India's caste system, yet they all had long-standing preferences for light skin, especially in women. Japanese women have fled the sun, covered up, and used white pancake makeup for centuries. When Europeans and Americans first came to Japan in the middle of the nineteenth century, Japanese artists usually depicted the visitors as white or off-white, the same color they used for upper-class Japanese. Sometimes they portrayed the foreigners, even wealthy people, as tan, the color they would assign to Japanese peasants who worked all day in the sun.[6]

This is not just old history in Japan. Two sisters were born in the 1960s. The first bore dark features. Her grandparents, immediately upon her birth, reacted negatively, saying, "She is dark and therefore ugly." After her younger sister was born with lighter skin, the grandparents said of this newborn, "She is pretty and will marry well." The older sister heard repeatedly throughout childhood that her dark skin made her ugly. She felt bitter about this well into the fifth decade of her life[7]. For the most part, colorism in Asia is a class imperative. Like Scarlett O'Hara in *Gone With the Wind*, to be light is to be rich, for dark skin comes from working outside in the sun. The yearning to be light is a desire to look like rich Asians, not like Whites.[8]

That class imperative carries over into Asian America. Sociologist Rebecca King-O'Riain rebuts the idea that Asian Americans, in seeking lighter skin, are trying to look like White people. She studied Japanese American beauty pageants and had this to say about the color issue in that context:

> The pageant then was a place where Japanese standards of beauty were affirmed and even enforced. For example, all the pageants I studied had a no tanning rule. They asked the participants not to get too dark and some women were rumored in the past to have been disqualified for tanning. The meaning of this [was] that . . . a Japanese sense of beauty, i.e., not being too dark because it means that you are "lower class" or work outside for a living, was valued over the more "majority" beauty belief in a dark tanned body. The argument that many people gave me was that being too dark makes the candidates look bad in kimono and that "lighter" skin is "better for Japanese." One candidate, who was naturally very dark, was warned to be really careful about tanning. She tried desperately to make her skin as light as possible and told me that she had rubbed lemons on her face at one point to try to lighten her skin. "They told us not to tan. (Why?) Because dark in Japanese means . . . you are the peasant class. You work in the fields. In American society the darker you are, the fuller your lips are is what you really want to look like. It hasn't moved into the Japanese community. They still want you to be fair and light." In addition, the negative association with darkness is probably also related to Japanese American attitudes toward dark skin also found in Japan, i.e., Okinawans are "dark" therefore considered poor, uncouth, and undesirable, as well as in the United States. This is probably reinforced by the assumption that lighter skin is associated with not only higher racial, but also class, status. Japanese Americans had their own colorism standards then and did not just adapt

majority standards from a white dominant society. They were not just blindly mimicking whiteness standards of beauty. With this emphasis on "lighter" being better by Japanese standards, this did not mean that half "white" candidates [for queen] did better because they were lighter. In fact, many found that indeed, they were too white. . . .

No Eyelid Glue, Nasal Inserts or Whitening Cream Here
Finally, some mixed race candidates actually tried to alter their physical appearance to appear more Japanese. . . . For example, some of the women dyed their hair dark black instead of their natural brown to appear more Japanese. Others used eyeliner to make their eyes appear more almond shaped or used colored contacts to make their eyes brown instead of blue.[9]

The Philippines may be something of an unusual case among Asian nations in that there, color hierarchies may have an element of reaching after Whiteness to them. Alone among Asian nations, the Philippines endured more than three centuries of Spanish colonial rule. During that time, the colonial masters built an elaborate hierarchy of race, class, and color not unlike those the Spanish constructed in Latin America. The ruling racial class were Iberian Spaniards. The people they called *indios* inhabited the lowest reaches of society. In between were various degrees of mestizos, depending mainly on color and wealth but also on the degree of Spanish versus Chinese ancestry that was mixed with Filipino. Thus, there is a quality of orientation to European-derived features and status to Filipino colorism that is missing from other Asian colorism. It may not be that Filipinos who yearned for lighter skin were wishing to be White, but certainly they were wishing to look like members of the Filipino upper class, who were mestizo.[10]

It seems likely that, for most Asian Americans, the impulse toward lightness has both indigenous Asian class roots and also a colonial or postcolonial Whiteness element laid over it. Undoubtedly, every Asian society exhibited a preference for light-skinned beauty, especially among women, before serious encounters with Europeans and Americans in the modern era. Just as certainly, in the last half century there has grown up an international celebrity culture made up largely of models and movie stars and a concomitant international beauty culture, which has favored Whiteness. As will be seen in chapters 3 and 4, Asian Americans, immigrants especially, who show a preference for light skin articulate their desire in old-country class terms. But it is argued in chapter 4 that behind that class desire lies a yearning to be seen as the ideal Asian in the eyes of White people—a Whiteness move.

There is almost no scholarship on colorism among Asian Americans. The only article published thus far is "Skin-Color Preferences and Body Satisfaction Among South Asian-Canadian and European-Canadian Female University Students," by Sarita Sahay and Niva Piran. After interviewing

Figure 1.1.   Chinese mestizos in the Philippines in the mid-nineteenth century.   Image from Jean Mallat de Bassilan, *Les Philippines* (Paris, 1846).

one hundred South Asian women and one hundred with European ancestors at the University of Toronto, they concluded that the majority of the South Asian women had a strong desire to be lighter than they were but that they did not desire to be White. Conversely, the European-descended women still wanted to be White but most wished to be darker—more tanned—than they were. Medium-toned and darker South Asian women expressed more general dissatisfaction with their bodies than did light-skinned women.[11]

Such information is important, but it is barely a beginning. It does not go so far, in fact, as this analysis of the colorism phenomenon, culled from an undergraduate paper written by a Cambodian American woman who asked to remain unnamed:

"Don't stay out in the sun too long! You'll get dark and never find a husband!" Since I was young, skin tone has always been an indication of a social and ethnically Asian hierarchy. It was believed that the lighter the skin, the more appealing and attractive the person. It was a characteristic of rich, learned, and educated people who did not need to labor outside and toil in the sun. Another broad interpretation of colorism, a form of racism, should be applied to the general scope of Asian ethnic hierarchy within the Asian community, where lighter-skinned Asians such as Chinese, Koreans, and Japanese are held more highly than Southeast Asians or Pilipinos. . . .

When I was growing up, my parents had instilled in me the notion that I was prettier as a light-skinned child than when I had gotten darker as a teenager. . . . When I decided to attend UCSB, the sun exposure and coastal location provoked my parents to remind me to stay away from the sun.

A Filipina American student, Joy Ipac, wrote:

My grandmother would say how beautiful my sister and I were because of our light skin, long straight hair, and somewhat pointed noses (not flat). My grandmother would talk about Filipinos having flat noses and how that wasn't very attractive. She's pinched my nose and said you're lucky you didn't get that much of a flat Filipino nose. . . . There are products that they sell to whiten your skin color. A lot of my friends who had the darker skin pigment would use this product to try and whiten their skin. I had a couple of friends who were really dark in skin color and they'd tell me how their parents would say that they're so dark and would constantly remind them not to stay in the sun so long, or just to wear hats so they don't get any darker than they already are.

Chrissy Lau, who is Chinese American, wrote this:

When I was young, I used to be very dark. I used to swim every day and spend a lot of time under the sun. Naturally, I got tanned and became very dark. One day, my mother yelled at me with disgust and said, "Look how dark you are! You're becoming black!" I could not understand why she was yelling at me because I was dark. She knew I loved to go swimming, and she knew I was having fun. She's the one who let me go swimming in the first place. What's the big deal if I am dark? But it was actually a bigger deal than I thought it was. My mother followed the value of light skin and didn't want to have a dark daughter who would be "ugly." This incident made me realize that dark skin equaled to ugly and light skin equaled to pretty. With factors including the desire to look beautiful and the inclination to please my mother, I stopped swimming in my later years of childhood. I didn't want to be tanned because I didn't want to look "black," as my mother put it. I began to form a prejudice that I found light skin to be more attractive than dark skin, not only within the Asian race, but the Black race and the Hispanic race. It was as if I had stolen my mom's pair of glasses and began wearing them.

Growing up, my family also emphasized the beauty of eyes. Big eyes were beautiful and small eyes were ugly. . . . Within my extended family on my mother's side, they all have big eyes. Unluckily, I have small eyes. I got my small eyes from my dad. . . . When I was little, I would hear comments about whose eyes were beautiful. . . . I remember my aunts and Grandmother just complimenting family members about their big eyes, and they would never compliment me or say anything to me. In a way, they looked down on me and felt sorry for me because I did not have big eyes. I wished with all my heart that I had big eyes just so that I could receive one of those compliments. I used to think: if only I had big eyes then I would be beautiful. I found myself judging others and seeing if they had big eyes, especially Asian people. . . . I literally grew up with this colorism, and it was not until I recently attended college that I learned that this was not true. People are beautiful no matter whatever features they have, big eyes or little eyes.

Yenyy Sihapanya, who is Laotian American, wrote this:

Laotians have a term [that] refers to a dark peasant girl or a girl from the country or farmland. The term is often used to mean a stupid, clumsy, and uncivilized person. The term is used to describe a person when they make a mistake or cause an accident. One is also labeled with this title in a joking manner when others want to demean one. . . .

At 22 years old, I seriously fought with my mother for the first time because she did not like my boyfriend simply because he was dark. It never mattered to her who he was or that his family was of a higher class. Because we were lighter skinned Asians, we were better and she did not want me to be with him. She and my father admitted this to me without shame or any reservation.

I know that my mother would prefer it if I had bigger eyes. She teased me as a child that I had Chinese eyes and that I was not beautiful because of them. She, and her two sisters in the [United States] and Canada, have all had eyelid surgery.

Most, if not all, of my mother's Laotian friends have also had the same procedures done. My mother has mentioned and offered to pay for me to have my eyelids done. They all believe that bigger eyes are more beautiful. . . . My mother never said that White people's eyes are prettier, just that big eyes are pretty. But we all know that White people have big eyes. . . . [N]o one has ever said that they want to look White. Then again, what community will openly admit to such prejudices. . . . I think that we all just know.

Sunny Yang, a Korean American woman, had this to say:

Ever since I could remember, my parents always encouraged my sister and me not to tan. They always said we looked like a Black person or a country bumpkin when we got dark. The meaning behind this [un]flattering comment was that we looked like lower-class people. In Korea, lighter skin color was more desirable as marriage material than darker skin color because it represented the status of the person throughout history. In Korea, a long time ago, either you were an aristocrat or a servant. The servants worked outside in the sun and were dark and uneducated, while the rich aristocrats were busy studying indoors memorizing the books and wore clothes that covered them from head to toe. . . .

My father used to call me "Snow White" while he would call my sister "Dark Princess." Even though, according to him, we were both princesses, we knew there was a hierarchy. Somehow, as little children, we understood that being lighter was better. This never bothered me because I was the lighter of the two, but I guess it bothered my sister. My sister, even to this date, hates getting dark and always compares herself to me. One day, I remember her pointing out that she was lighter than [me], due to staying away from the sun exposure. She seemed very satisfied with it. . . .

Most of the Korean American females I knew always wore makeup foundation a shade lighter than their skin tone, including myself, because light skin was thought to be more beautiful than dark skin. The desire for lighter skin was so great that what one saw in the mirror was influenced to the point of not seeing straight. I must say, I looked quite ridiculous when I saw the pictures of my ghostly white face.

It is clear that there are issues here of vital importance to the self-concept and happiness of Asian Americans—women in particular—as well as to their interactions with other people within their ethnic communities.

COLORISM IN BLACK AND WHITE

Colorism in the United States is hardly an issue for Asian Americans only. In fact, the shape and effects of colorism in other populations have received a much greater volume of study than has colorism among Asian Americans. The colorism phenomenon in the United States has roots deep in the historical experiences of African-descended people here. At the time they first came to North America, Africans may have been a mixed multitude of ethnic groups, but they were ancestrally unmixed with non-Africans. Soon, however, Whites, Blacks, and Indians mingled and mated on the North American continent. In the colonial era, much of that mixing was between African and Indian slaves and White indentured servants who shared neighboring class positions and social proximity. Both genders were involved from each racial group. Between the time of the American Revolution and the Civil War, more often it was men of the master racial class—slave masters and overseers, for the most part—who visited their attentions on slave women. Often these were rapes, and even in cases where sturdy relationships were built, there was usually still an element of compulsion. Such unions begat children who exhibited mixed features: hair, skin, and eyes that were lighter than unmixed Africans and darker than unmixed Europeans.[12]

Thus there arose a group of people within slavery who were racially mixed, who bore visible marks of White ancestry along with Black or Indian. The master class drew a line between themselves and such mixed people. This has often been called the one-drop rule: one "drop" of Black "blood"—one known African ancestor—made one Black and a slave. White blood, or known European ancestry, seems not to have been so powerful in determining one's class position, servitude, or life chances. One could be part-White and still be assigned to the Black racial category, but one could not be part-Black and still be assigned to the White racial category. The one-drop rule masked racial mixture. It was an effective way for the master to get away with racialized sexual abuse without consequences, and for the master's White children to ignore claims of family that might come from their part-Black half-brothers and -sisters.[13]

As Stephen Small persuasively argues, most mixed people remained slaves despite their part-European ancestry and features.[14] Yet some mixed individuals enjoyed a modicum of privilege within slavery based on their part-White ancestry. A small number of masters lived quasi-married lives with slave concubines and their mixed children. Some such children enjoyed relative freedom so long as their fathers lived. Some learned to read and write, which were privileges denied by law and custom to most slaves. A few gained freedom. The free Black population was lighter and more European-featured than the slave population, on the average. Even within slavery, a certain social value came to reside in Blacks, especially women, who possessed lighter skin and eyes and more European features. New Orleans was famous for its Quadroon Ball, where light-skinned, mixed-race women (both slave and semi-free) were paraded by their rich White paramours. Despite racial limitations that placed them beneath Whites, such women possessed status and wealth that could not be approached by other, darker, African-descended women.

Once the slave institution was formally repudiated, the leadership cohort in African America was made up at first mainly of former free Blacks and their descendants, for it was they who possessed the education, capital, and leadership skills to take charge. From P.B.S. Pinchback and Archibald Grimké in slavery's aftermath; to Charles W. Chesnutt, Alonzo Herndon, and Azalia Hackley at the turn of the century; to W.E.B. Du Bois, Mary Church Terrell, and Walter White in the first third of the twentieth century; to Adam Clayton Powell, Edward Brooke, and Julian Bond in the 1950s and 1960s, a disproportionate number of African Americans of power, wealth, and social prominence bore visible evidence of mixed ancestry. Thus colorism—the preference for light skin, aquiline noses, thin lips, and "good hair"—among African-descended Americans has its roots in a Whiteness move and a class move at once. Colorism did not necessarily represent an attempt to look like Whites. The desire was mainly (at least before the 1980s) to look like the leaders and monied class of African Americans, most of whom possessed significant White ancestry.[15]

Those two issues—class identity and racial physicality—are the major features of colorism for African Americans. There is a large, carefully constructed, social scientific literature on the consequences of colorism in terms of class status and life chances for African Americans. Even when one controls for such background factors as education and parents' class status, African Americans with lighter skin tone earn more money than darker African Americans. Lighter people complete more years of education. They have higher occupational status and so do their spouses. They enjoy more integrated housing options and a wider range of occupational choices. They have fewer mental health problems and higher self-esteem. In fact, Michael Hughes and Bradley Hertel found that "the impact of skin color on socioeconomic status among black Americans [is] as great as the impact of race (black-white) on socioeconomic status in American society."[16]

Charles Johnson, Lloyd Warner, Buford Junker, and Walter Adams began to consider the psychological consequences of skin color in two groundbreaking studies published in 1941 by the American Council on Education. They interviewed several hundred rural Southern and urban Midwestern African Americans about their attitudes toward skin color, hair, and facial features and the connections of those attitudes to self-esteem and other personality characteristics. These were monumental studies with complex findings, but the scholars found a simple consensus among African Americans: lighter was better than darker, European features better than African ones, straight hair better than nappy. Darker skin and African features were associated with evil, poverty, lack of education, crudeness, laziness, violence, and lack of sophistication. Lighter skin and more European features connoted the opposite.[17]

These opinions took a toll on the psyches of dark women and girls, especially. A little girl named Marie was told regularly by her grandmother, "You'll have to take care of your skin and make yourself attractive, because you are so dark." Her mother recalled, "One day Marie hugged and kissed me and said, 'Mama, nobody loves me because I am black.'" Sometimes one feature partially compensated for another, as in the observation, "She is dark but has good hair and keen features." So to be dark was bad in most Black people's eyes. But did it follow that African Americans wanted to be White? Interviews conducted by Johnson and E. Franklin Frazier revealed lots of people wanting to be as light as possible and to associate with light people, but they did not want to be White or even to become more acceptable to White people. Rather, their interest was to achieve status within Black communities. As Bonnie Allen put it, "I've never really believed we were trying to look white, because I've met few Blacks who truly wished they were white. We were simply trying to look like that color of Black people who were supposedly getting over."[18]

Throughout the middle decades of the twentieth century, the cosmetic industry marketed harsh chemical skin lighteners and hair straighteners in African American magazines such as *Ebony* and *Jet*. Models and actresses almost always possessed light skin and aquiline noses. This declined for a time in the latter 1960s and 1970s when the Black Power movement asserted the beauty of dark skin, wide noses, thick lips, and kinky hair. But by the 1980s that advocacy of dark beauty had declined, and light was beautiful once again. And the light, straight-haired models were back in the magazines.

Recent decades have seen an outpouring of writing on the phenomenon of African American beauty. It echoes the themes that Johnson, et al., struck in the 1940s. African Americans—mainly women, but also men to some degree—have yearned after skin and features that were lighter and more European-looking than the average among African Americans. Perceiving oneself as beautiful in these terms seems to have been intimately related to how positively one viewed oneself.[19] Among the most careful and systematic are Margaret Hunter, Maxine Thompson, and Verna Keith. Thompson and Keith found that "skin tone has negative effects on both self-esteem and self-efficacy"—one's sense of competence. Men were more affected in the area of self-efficacy; lighter men felt more confident in the business and professional world than darker men. Women were more affected in the area of self-esteem, with darker women suffering badly for their skin color.[20]

Hunter analyzed women's bodies as manipulable commodities and color as social capital:

Beauty is a crucial resource for women because it operates as a form of social capital. It is transformable into other types of capital, through access to high status occupations, higher educational attainment, and even higher incomes. . . . [B]y the 1980s, when women had made significant inroads into corporations and management positions, beauty became as important as intellectual qualifications for employment.

Beauty as capital operates similarly to [Cheryl] Harris's conception of "whiteness as property." . . . I suggest that beauty operates as a form of capital much in the way that whiteness does.

In this economic context women's bodies are manipulable commodities objectified for male consumption. More specifically, the entire beauty industry is built on the foundational principle that women will alter their bodies, through make[up], colored contact lenses, body hair removal, and plastic surgery to increase their amount of beauty, or capital. The racial implications are obvious. Women of color, like White women, spend millions of dollars every year on beauty products. However, unlike White women's products, many products for women of color are geared toward whitening as a part of the beautifying process. Hair straighteners, light colored contacts, and even some skin creams and bleaches all help women of color become more beautiful by becoming more White. Cosmetic surgery is also a tool used by many to whiten and beautify.[21]

It is possible, however, that a Black person can be too light. One should approximate White, or at least upper-class Black, standards of beauty as nearly as possible, but there is a price to be paid for "trying to be White." In mid-century Black America, a light person was referred to as "yellow," and it was often said that "A yellow person will sell us out every time." Hunter observes that "light skin is associated with Whites, assimilation, and a lack of racial consciousness, thus leaving some light skinned people to feel unwelcome in their own communities. This is a dilemma of ethnic authenticity. . . . a feeling that one is, or is not, 'Black enough.' . . . Light skinned people . . . report feeling like outsiders, unaccepted, or even pushed out of their own communities and community organizations based on skin tone." There are associations, then, of ethnic inauthenticity, even betrayal, that may accompany light skin, silky hair, and sharp features.[22]

AND BROWN

Writers who study non-Black peoples of color in the United States are beginning to look at colorism in other communities. Students of Latinos in the United States rightly point out that Latinos are not a single group but many and that they or their ancestors came from places with a variety of racial systems. Yet there are certain commonalities among Latin American racial systems and common distinctions from the U.S. system, all of which set up colorism to be an issue for Latinos in the United States. As Clara Rodríguez notes, by contrast with the U. S. binary racial system:

> [I]n Latin America, racial constructions have tended to be more fluid and based on many variables, like social class and phenotype. There also have been many, often overlapping, categories, and mixtures have been consistently acknowledged and have had their own terminology. . . . At the same time, pigmentation was emphasized, and implicit and sometimes explicit racism dominated the determination of one's social status.[23]

In their Latin American countries of origin, people often think of such distinctions as class hierarchies that use elements of color and phenotype as a marking mechanism. But, according to Rodríguez, "When they migrate to the United States, some Latinos become more aware of the racism existing in their own country of origin." The racism at the core of even the seemingly multicultural concept of *mestizaje* is clear: "Even those countries that subscribe to a racial ideology of mestizaje often maintain racial and class hierarchies that favor upper-class interests and political agendas, privilege European components, ignore racialisms, and neutralize expressions of pluralism by indigenous or African-descended groups."[24]

Sociologists have found several axes of light color privilege among Chicanos and other Latinos. Carlos Arce, Edward Murguia, and Parker Frisbie found that "Mexican Americans with a European physical appearance . . . have more enhanced life chances as measured by higher socioeconomic status than Mexican Americans with an indigenous Native American physical appearance." Murguia and Edward Telles break it down further: "Chicanos with a darker and Native American phenotype receive significantly lower earnings than those of a lighter and more European phenotype." And "[T]he lightest skin-toned and most European-looking quarter of the Mexican American population had about 1.5 more years of schooling than the darker and more Indian-looking majority. Differences in schooling by phenotype persisted with and without controls for other factors." Luis Vásquez, Enedina García-Vásquez, Sheri Bauman, and Arturo Sierra found that "students with the darkest skin had significantly lower levels of acculturation than those with lighter skin." There is even some evidence that dark Chicano men suffer from depression more than light Chicano men.[25]

Novelist Julia Álvarez describes the way many Latinas have experienced colorism issues in her autobiographical essay, "A White Woman of Color":

> Growing up in the Dominican Republic, I experienced racism within my own family—though I didn't think of it as racism. But there was definitely a hierarchy of beauty, which was the main currency in our daughters-only

family. It was not until years later, from the vantage point of this country and this education that I realized that this hierarchy of beauty was dictated by our coloring. We were a progression of whitening, as if my mother were slowly bleaching the color out of her children.

The oldest sister had the darkest coloring, with very curly hair and "coarse" features. She looked the most like Papi's side of the family and was considered the least pretty. I came next, with "good hair," and skin that back then was a deep olive, for I was a tomboy—another dark mark against me—who would not stay out of the sun. The sister right after me had my skin color, but she was a good girl who stayed indoors, so she was much paler, her hair a golden brown. But the pride and joy of the family was the baby. She was the one who made heads turn and strangers approach asking to feel her silken hair. She was white white, an adjective that was repeated in describing her color as if to deepen the shade of white. Her eyes were brown, but her hair was an unaccountable towheaded blond.

Álvarez makes clear that in her Dominican family and community, preference for light skin and small features drew on class hierarchies and a desire by many to deny the African part of their inheritance. Álvarez herself was light enough that "All I had to do was stay out of the sun and behave myself and I could pass as a pretty white girl."[26]

THIS BOOK

So colorism has been documented and analyzed for African Americans and Latinos by many scholars over several decades. For Asian Americans, such an exploration is just beginning. The feature of Asian American colorism that immediately stands out as being somewhat different from the Black and Latino versions is that Asian American colorism seems not to be mainly about Whiteness at its point of origin. For Asian Americans, color hierarchies seem to be as deeply rooted in old-country class distinctions—in the desire to look like upper-class Asians who did not have to do body work out in the sun—as in U. S.-generated desires to look like White people.

This book, *Is Lighter Better?*, is a preliminary exploration. In it, observations are made; patterns suggested; and possible explanations are posited. The goal of the book, however, is to provoke frank discussion and further research that will (before long) inform, reshape, and even supplant the work done here.

More than most books, *Is Lighter Better?* is the product of group effort. Its inspiration came from issues students raised persistently in Asian American Studies 137, "Multiethnic Asian Americans," a course Paul Spickard taught for many years at the University of California, Santa Barbara. Some of those students and Spickard planned this study. Together they designed the interview survey that is the basis of chapter 3. They recruited some colleagues to contribute to chapters 2, 4, and 5. Meanwhile, Joanne Rondilla was working, in the ethnic studies department at UC Berkeley and the cosmetics department at Nordstrom, on the ways beauty culture and the cosmetics industry act on Asian American women.

The authors of the personal stories in chapter 2—Robin Le, Charmaine Tuason, Marybeth Liu, Sara Cruz, Luz Devadason, and Karen Jackson—are listed at the start of each of their contributions. Spickard drafted chapter 3, based on research conducted by Monica Chum, Holly Hoegi, Lynn Kawabe, Akshata Mankikar, Spickard, Charmaine Tuason, and Mey Year. Rondilla drafted chapter 4, with research assistance by Lilynda Agvateesiri. Rondilla drafted chapter 5, with research assistance by Sara Cruz and Christie Trieu. Spickard drafted the introduction, and both Spickard and Rondilla drafted the epilogue. Spickard served as first editor of the entire manuscript. Rondilla made the second round of editorial revisions. Then all the contributing researchers and writers read and offered suggestions. Thus, while Rondilla and Spickard had the largest roles in the final manuscript and so are listed as primary authors, *Is Lighter Better?* is the intellectual product of all the authors listed here.

Is Lighter Better? is organized as follows. In chapter 2, "The Darker and Lighter Sister," six young women describe their struggles with colorism. Three are relatively dark women who have experienced pain at the hands of other Asian Americans. Three are lighter than the average Asian American, as they have some White ancestry. The six women have different voices and experiences, but all of their lives have been deeply affected by the color of their skin and the connotations that others have laid on them.

Chapter 3 describes an interview survey we took of ninety-nine Asian American women and men. They ranged in age from sixteen to eighty-two and included representatives of all the major Asian American ethnic groups. Some were immigrants, others American-born people ranging to the fourth generation. They told about their feelings with regard to skin color, eye shape, body type, and other beauty and identity issues. The interviewers explored with them their personal preferences and the issues they have witnessed among other Asian Americans.

Chapter 4, "Making a Better Me?," explores the cosmetics industry's relationship to Asian American women. In particular, it focuses on the target marketing of skin lighteners to Asian American women, the responses of women to this marketing campaign, and the physical and psychological consequences of their use of such products.

Chapter 5, "The Unkindest Cut," describes the ways that Asian American women have interacted with the cosmetic surgery industry. It finds many of the same dynamics at work in the marketing and consumption of cosmetic surgery as are used in the selling and applying of skin lighteners: an attempt to appear White masked by a rhetoric that appeals to some supposedly race-neutral standard of beauty. As with the skin lighteners, so too with the cosmetic surgery, the psychological and physical consequences for women are sometimes devastating.

NOTES

1. Throughout this book we capitalize racial names: Asian, Native American, White, Black, and so forth. Black and White are not, in this usage, descriptive adjectives; they are proper nouns and adjectives. When we refer to actual colors, we do not capitalize.

2. Cedric Herring, "Skin Deep: Race and Complexion in the 'Color Blind' Era," in *Skin/Deep: How Race and Complexion Matter in the "Color-Blind" Era*, ed. Cedric Herring, Verna M. Keith, and Hayward Derrick Horton (Urbana: University of Illinois Press, 2004), 1–21.

3. *Mississippi Masala*, directed by Mira Nair, SCS Films, Columbia TriStar Home Video, 1992; Charmaine Tuason, Untitled student paper (University of California, Santa Barbara, July 2003).

4. V. S. Naipaul, *Half a Life* (New York: Knopf, 2001), 12–13.

5. Naipaul, *Half a Life*, 24, 33, 34, 40, 44.

6. Sadao Kikuchi, *A Treasury of Japanese Wood Block Prints: Ukiyo-E*, trans. Don Kenny (New York: Crown, 1969), plates 18–59; Ann Yonemura, *Yokohama: Prints from Nineteenth-Century Japan* (Washington, D.C.: Arthur M. Sackler Gallery, Smithsonian Institution, 1990); Michael Cooper, ed., *They Came to Japan: An Anthology of European Reports on Japan, 1543–1640* (1965; repr., Ann Arbor: University of Michigan Center for Japanese Studies, 1995), 37–38;

7. Personal communication with Paul Spickard.

8. Hiroshi Wagatsuma, "The Social Perception of Skin Color in Japan," *Daedalus* 96, no. 2 (1967): 407–43.

9. Rebecca Chiyoko King-O'Riain, *Race Work: Body, Culture, and Japanese American Beauty Pageants* (Minneapolis: University of Minnesota Press, 2006), chapter 4 (manuscript copy courtesy of the publisher).

10. Edgar Wickberg, *The Chinese in Philippine Life, 1850–1898* (New Haven, CT: Yale University Press, 1965); Edgar Wickberg, "The Chinese Mestizo in Philippine History," *Journal of Southeast Asian History* 5 (1964): 62–100.

11. Sarita Sahay and Niva Piran, "Skin-Color Preferences and Body Satisfaction Among South Asian-Canadian and European-Canadian Female University Students," *Journal of Social Psychology* 137, no. 2 (1997): 161–71.

12. Paul R. Spickard, *Mixed Blood: Intermarriage and Ethnic Identity in Twentieth-Century America* (Madison: University of Wisconsin Press, 1989), 235–52; G. Regi-

nald Daniel, "Either Black or White: Race, Modernity, and the Law of the Excluded Middle," in *Racial Thinking in the United States*, ed. Paul Spickard and G. Reginald Daniel (Notre Dame, IN: University of Notre Dame Press, 2004), 21–59; G. Reginald Daniel, *More Than Black? Multiracial Identity and the New Racial Order* (Philadelphia: Temple University Press, 2002), 1–45; Joel Williamson, *New People: Miscegenation and Mulattoes in the United States* (New York: Macmillan, 1980); F. James Davis, *Who Is Black? One Nation's Definition* (University Park: Pennsylvania State University Press, 1991); Winthrop D. Jordan, "American Chiaroscuro: The Status and Definition of Mulattoes in the British Colonies," *William and Mary Quarterly* 3rd ser., 19 (1962), 183–200; Winthrop D. Jordan, *White Over Black: American Attitudes Toward the Negro, 1550–1812* (Chapel Hill: University of North Carolina Press, 1968), 136–78; James F. Brooks, ed., *Confounding the Color Line: The Indian-Black Experience in North America* (Lincoln: University of Nebraska Press, 2002).

13. G. Reginald Daniel, "Passers and Pluralists: Subverting the Racial Divide," in *Racially Mixed People in America*, ed. Maria P. P. Root (Newbury Park, CA: Sage, 1992), 91–107; Winthrop D. Jordan, "The One-Drop Rule," manuscript courtesy of the author (2004); Martha Hodes, *White Women, Black Men: Illicit Sex in the 19th-Century South* (New Haven, CT: Yale University Press, 1997).

14. Stephen A. Small, "Mustefinos Are White by Law: Whites and People of Mixed Racial Origins in Historical and Comparative Perspective," in *Racial Thinking in the United States*, ed. Spickard and Daniel, 60–79; Ira Berlin, *Slaves Without Masters: The Free Negro in the Antebellum South* (New York: Knopf, 1974), 108–32; E. Franklin Frazier, *Black Bourgeoisie: The Rise of a New Middle Class* (New York: Free Press, 1957); E. Franklin Frazier, *The Negro Family in the United States* (1939; repr., Notre Dame, IN: University of Notre Dame Press, 2001), 182–245; Donald L. Horowitz, "Color Differentiation in the American Systems of Slavery," *Journal of Interdisciplinary History* 3, no. 3 (1973): 509–41; Robert L. Harris, Jr., "Charleston's Free Afro-American Elite," *South Carolina Historical Magazine* 82, no. 4 (1981): 289–310; Robert Brent Toplin, "Between Black and White: Attitudes Toward Southern Mulattoes, 1830–1861," *Journal of Southern History* 45, no. 2 (1979): 185–200; Walter White, *Flight* (1926; repr., Baton Rouge: Louisiana State University Press, 1998).

15. Frazier, *Black Bourgeoisie*; Williamson, *New People*; Paul Spickard, "The Power of Blackness: Mixed-Race Leaders and the Monoracial Ideal," in *Racial Thinking in the United States*, ed. Spickard and Daniel, 103–23; Spickard, *Mixed Blood*, 317–24; W. E. Burghardt Du Bois, *Dusk of Dawn: An Essay Toward an Autobiography of a Race Concept* (1940; repr., New Brunswick, N.J.: Transaction, 1984); Willard B. Gatewood, *Aristocrats of Color: The Black Elite, 1880–1920* (Bloomington: Indiana University Press, 1990); Edward Byron Reuter, *The Mulatto in the United States* (1918; repr. New York: Negro Universities Press, 1969), 166–215; Lawrence Otis Graham, *Our Kind of People: Inside America's Black Upper Class* (New York: Harper Collins, 1999); Dorothy West, *The Wedding* (New York: Doubleday, 1995).

16. Michael Hughes and Bradley R. Hertel, "The Significance of Color Remains: A Study of Life Chances, Mate Selection, and Ethnic Consciousness Among Black Americans," *Social Forces* 68, no. 4 (1990): 1105–20; Herring, "Skin Deep"; Margaret Hunter, "Light, Bright, and Almost White: The Advantages and Disadvantages of

Light Skin," in *Skin/Deep*, ed. Herring, Keith, and Horton, 22–44; Kathy Russell, Midge Wilson, and Ronald Hall, *The Color Complex: The Politics of Skin Color Among African Americans* (New York: Harcourt Brace Jovanovich, 1992), 24–40, 124–34; Verna M. Keith and Cedric Herring, "Skin Tone and Stratification in the Black Community," *American Journal of Sociology* 97, no. 3 (1991): 760–78; Howard E. Freeman, J. Michael Ross, David Armor, and Thomas F. Pettigrew, "Color Gradation and Attitudes among Middle-Income Negroes," *American Sociological Review* 31, no. 3 (1966): 365–74; H. Edward Ransford, "Skin Color, Life Chances, and Anti-White Attitudes," *Social Problems* 18 (1970): 164–79; Mark E. Hill, "Color Differences in the Socioeconomic Status of African American Men: Results of a Longitudinal Study," *Social Forces* 78, no. 4 (2000): 1437–60; Maxine S. Thompson and Verna M. Keith, "The Blacker the Berry: Gender, Skin Tone, Self-Esteem, and Self-Efficacy," *Gender and Society* 15, no. 3 (2001): 336–57; Ozzie L. Edwards, "Skin Color as a Variable in Racial Attitudes of Black Urbanites," *Journal of Black Studies* 3, no. 4 (1972): 473–83; Jo Holtzman, "Color Caste Changes among Black College Students," *Journal of Black Studies* 4, no. 1 (1973): 92–101; Richard Seltzer and Robert C. Smith, "Color Differences in the Afro-American Community and the Differences They Make," *Journal of Black Studies* 21, no. 3 (1991): 279–86.

17. Charles S. Johnson, *Growing Up in the Black Belt: Negro Youth in the Rural South* (1941; repr., New York: Schocken, 1970); W. Lloyd Warner, Buford H. Junker, and Walter A. Adams, *Color and Human Nature: Negro Personality Development in a Northern City* (1941; repr., New York: Harper and Row, 1969).

18. Warner, et al., *Color and Human Nature*, 14–16; Johnson, *Growing Up in the Black Belt*, 258–63; E. Franklin Frazier Papers, Moorland-Springarn Research Center, Howard University, Washington, D.C., box 82, no. 11; box 92, no. 78; Spickard, *Mixed Blood*, 318–19; Bonnie Allen, "It Ain't Easy Being Pinky," *Essence* (July 1982), 67ff.

19. Selena Bond and Thomas F. Cash, "Black Beauty: Skin Color and Body Images among African-American College Women," *Journal of Applied Social Psychology* 22 (1992): 874–88; Ayana Byrd and Lori L. Tharps, *Hair Story: Untangling the Roots of Black Hair in America* (New York: St. Martin's, 2001); Thomas F. Cash and Nancy C. Duncan, "Physical Attractiveness Stereotyping among Black American College Students," *Journal of Social Psychology* 122 (1984): 71–77; John W. Chambers, Jr., Tangela Clark, Leatha Dantzler, and Joseph A. Baldwin, "Perceived Attractiveness, Facial Features, and African Self-Consciousness," *Journal of Black Psychology* 20, no. 3 (1994): 305–24; Stephanie Irby Coard, Alfiee M. Breland, and Patricia Raskin, "Perceptions of and Preferences for Skin Color, Black Racial Identity, and Self-Esteem among African Americans," *Journal of Applied Social Psychology* 31 (2001): 2256–75; Angela R. Gillem and Cathy A. Thompson, eds., *Biracial Women in Therapy* (New York: Haworth Press, 2004); Aliona L. Gibson, *Nappy: Growing Up Black and Female in America* (New York: Harlem River Press, 1995); Kim Green, "The Pain of Living the Lye," *Essence* (June 1993): 38; Ronald Hall, "The Bleaching Syndrome: African Americans' Response to Cultural Domination Vis-à-Vis Skin Color," *Journal of Black Studies* 26, no. 2 (1995): 172–84; Aminifu R. Harvey, "The Issue of Skin Color in Psychotherapy with African Americans," *Families in Society*

(January 1995): 3–10; Tracy E. Hopkins, "The Darker the Berry," in *Testimony: Young African-Americans on Self-Discovery and Black Identity*, ed. Natasha Tarpley (Boston: Beacon, 1995), 231–35; Lisa Jones, *Bulletproof Diva: Tales of Race, Sex, and Hair* (New York: Doubleday, 1994); Obiagele Lake, *Blue Veins and Kinky Hair: Naming and Color Consciousness in African America* (Westport, CT: Praeger, 2003); Benilde Little, *Good Hair* (New York: Simon and Schuster, 1996); Douglas Longshore, "Color Connotations and Racial Attitudes," *Journal of Black Studies* 10, no. 2 (1979): 183–97; Angela M. Neal and Midge L. Wilson, "The Role of Skin Color and Features in the Black Community: Implications for Black Women and Therapy," *Clinical Psychology Review* 9 (1989): 323–33; Margo Okazawa-Rey, Tracey Robinson, and Janie Victoria Ward, "Black Women and the Politics of Skin Color and Hair," *Women and Therapy* 6 (1987): 89–102; Margo Okazawa-Rey, Tracey Robinson, and Janie Victoria Ward, "Black Women and the Politics of Skin Color and Hair," *Women's Studies Quarterly* 14, nos. 1–2 (1986): 13–14; Noliwe Makada Rooks, *Hair Raising: Beauty, Culture, and African American Women* (New Brunswick, N.J.: Rutgers University Press, 1996); Louie E. Ross, "Mate Selection Preferences among African American College Students," *Journal of Black Studies* 27, no. 4 (1997): 554–69; Russell, Wilson, and Hall, *Color Complex*; David Strutton, "Stereotypes of Black In-Group Attractiveness in Advertising: On Possible Psychological Effects," *Psychological Reports* 73 (1993): 507–11; J. Richard Udry, "The Importance of Being Beautiful: A Reexamination and Racial Comparison," *American Journal of Sociology* 83, no. 1 (1977): 154–60; J. Richard Udry, Karl E. Bauman, and Charles Chase, "Skin Color, Status, and Mate Selection," *American Journal of Sociology* 76, no. 1 (1971): 722–33; T. Joel Wade, "The Relationships Between Skin Color and Self-Perceived Global, Physical, and Sexual Attractiveness, and Self-Esteem for African Americans," *Journal of Black Psychology* 22, no. 3 (1996): 358–73; Jesse Washington, "A Lighter Shade of Black," *Essence* (January 1995), 40.

20. Maxine S. Thompson and Verna M. Keith, "The Blacker the Berry: Gender, Skin Tone, Self-Esteem, and Self-Efficacy," *Gender and Society* 15, no. 3 (2001): 336–57.

21. Margaret L. Hunter, "Light, Bright, and Almost White: The Advantages and Disadvantages of Light Skin," in *Skin/Deep*, ed. Herring, Keith, and Horton, 22–44. See also her "Colorstruck: Skin Color Stratification in the Lives of African American Women," *Sociological Inquiry* 68, no. 4 (1998): 517–35; "'If You're Light You're Alright': Light Skin Color as Social Capital for Women of Color," *Gender and Society* 16, no. 2 (2002): 175–93; and *Race, Gender, and the Politics of Skin Tone* (New York: Routledge, 2005). The concept of Whiteness as property comes from Cheryl Harris, "Whiteness as Property," *Harvard Law Review* 106 (1993).

22. Warner, Junker, and Adams, *Color and Human Nature*, 14; Hunter, "Light, Bright, and Almost White." See also K. Broussard, *What Looks Like Black* (Lincoln, NE: Universe, 2003).

23. Clara E. Rodríguez, *Changing Race: Latinos, the Census, and the History of Ethnicity in the United States* (New York: New York University Press, 2000), 9, 120.

24. Rodríguez, *Changing Race*, 10. In addition, *mestizaje* is often used to silence the voices of Native peoples and to mask the element of African heritage in the population. See Virginia Q. Tilley, "*Mestizaje* and the 'Ethnicization' of Race in Latin

America," in *Race and Nation: Ethnic Systems in the Modern World*, ed. Paul Spickard (New York: Routledge, 2005), 51–66.

25. Carlos H. Arce, Edward Murguia, and W. Parker Frisbie, "Phenotype and Life Chances Among Chicanos," *Hispanic Journal of Behavioral Sciences* 9, no. 1 (1987): 19–32; Edward E. Telles and Edward Murguia, "Phenotypic Discrimination and Income Differences among Mexican Americans," *Social Science Quarterly* 71, no. 4 (1990): 682–96; Edward Murguia and Edward E. Telles, "Phenotype and Schooling among Mexican Americans," *Sociology of Education* 69 (1996): 276–89; Luis A. Vásquez, Enedina García-Vásquez, Sheri A. Bauman, and Arturo S. Sierra, "Skin Color, Acculturation, and Community Interest Among Mexican American Students: A Research Note," *Hispanic Journal of Behavioral Sciences* 19, no. 3 (1997): 377–86; G. Edward Codina and Frank F. Montalvo, "Chicano Phenotype and Depression," *Hispanic Journal of Behavioral Sciences* 16, no. 3 (1994): 296–306. See also Hunter, *Politics of Skin Color*; Walter Allen, Edward Telles, and Margaret Hunter, "Skin Color, Income and Education: A Comparison of African Americans and Mexican Americans," *National Journal of Sociology* 12, no. 1 (2000): 129–80; John H. Relethford, Michael P. Stern, Sharon P. Gaskill, and Helen P. Hazuda, "Social Class, Admixture, and Skin Color Variation in Mexican Americans and Anglo-Americans Living in San Antonio, Texas," *American Journal of Physical Anthropology* 61 (1983): 97–102; Ronald E. Hall, "The 'Bleaching Syndrome': Implications of Light Skin for Hispanic American Assimilation," *Hispanic Journal of Behavioral Sciences* 16, no. 3 (1994), 307–14; Joseph P. Fitzpatrick, *Puerto Rican Americans* (Englewood Cliffs, N.J.: Prentice-Hall, 1971), 101–14.

26. Julia Álvarez, "A White Woman of Color," in *Half + Half: Writers on Growing Up Biracial and Bicultural*, ed. Claudine Chiawei O'Hearn (New York: Pantheon, 1998), 139–49.

· 2 ·

The Darker and Lighter Sister:
Telling Our Stories

In this chapter six young Asian American women tell their stories of life on the color line. Some are dark, some light. All have known times of self-doubt because of their appearance, often on account of other people's inability or unwillingness to see them clearly. Some of these women are hopeful, some melancholy, some resolute, some angry and defiant. All have come to points of resolution with regard to the color issues in their own lives.[1]

SELF-ACCEPTANCE by Robin Le

I am a second-generation Vietnamese American, born and raised with the notion that I carry the wrong shade of yellow. As a child, I grew up believing that being light skinned would categorize me as a pretty child. At the age of seven, I realized that I was too dark for my own ethnicity. I grew up being taunted with the words *my dang*, which translates into English as "*Black girl.*" It was not until I was thirteen that I realized that the color of my skin made me an outcast within the Asian American community. I was not good enough to be a part of their social sphere, because my complexion was a visible sign for them to place me as inferior. After years of torment over the pigment of my skin, I decided that drastic change must occur.

That summer, I was on medicated cream. The directions on the box warned me to avoid prolonged and excessive exposure to direct sunlight. Because I was a teenager, I could not care less what the directions warned. I would venture out into the yard and play with my neighbors. Within a matter of days, my face had a bad reaction to the sun. Tiny little pieces of skin began to peel, leaving lighter patches from the layer underneath. It did not take me long to realize that the cream would allow me to change the pigment of my skin and more importantly, the way people perceived me. So I used more of the cream. Day by day I would go out into the sun and at night, I would sit in front of the mirror and peel tiny pieces of skin off my face. After a long period of time, my face stopped reacting to the cream and sunlight. Only then did I realize that it was time to stop trying to change the color of who I was and to try to just embrace the fact that I would never be the shade of yellow that my mother so desired for me to be.

For years, it brought tears to my eyes when all I could see in the mirror was the reflection of a dark-pigmented girl who would never be accepted or embraced for who she is. I was a lost child wandering the world seeking self-acceptance. Because of the color of my skin, I was not Vietnamese or American enough. I was too dark to be Vietnamese and too dark to be the complexion that would allow me to be categorized with White Americans.

Eventually I came to acknowledge that I am who I am, but still the fact that my skin does not represent who I am saddens me. I no longer care to seek acceptance in the Vietnamese community, but I do wish that I were viewed as a Vietnamese person. Because of the pigment of my skin, people make the assumption that I am a Filipina, a Pacific Islander, a Latina, a half-breed Hapa, and the newest and latest one, an Eskimo. I wish who I am as a person was reflected in my looks.

Not long ago my friend called to tell me that his mother disapproved of his girlfriend because she was too dark. It was not enough for his mother that his girlfriend was intelligent and held a master's degree in psychology or that she came from a wealthy family within the same culture and heritage as his. His mother could not look past the color of his girlfriend's skin. His mother explained that all she wanted was for him to be with someone who looked as though she was from a higher class. She told him that she meant well, but how good can his mother's intentions be if she discriminates against a person based solely on how that person looks?

Another friend of mine has African American and Filipino parents. People tend to assume that she is just Black. She is far from just anything. I asked her how the color of her skin has affected the way people view her. She talked about how she attended an Asian American student conference at UC Irvine. An elderly Asian American man asked her if she was from south central Los Angeles. He said he was happy to see that there were other people of color besides Asians attending the conference. It turned out this man was the keynote speaker, a Korean American journalist who had covered the Los Angeles riots in 1992. I asked her whether she had clarified her identity for this man, but she said he was elderly and she did not want to embarrass him in front of everyone.

I disagree. That he is elderly does not justify his ignorant assumption. Feeling embarrassment is nothing if it is at the cost of making another person feel bad about his or her complexion. To change people's ignorant misconceptions about skin tone as the sole representation of who one is, we must take a stand and defend our heritage and culture. To change the world, we must start with one individual and have the hope that he or she, too, will change the mind of another human being. From this day forward, I shall refuse to allow the pigment of my skin to determine the sole representation of who I am as an individual. I will take responsibility for my own life and will have hope for renewal, change, and growth that I will one day be perceived the way I wish to be and not the way society has condemned me to be based on a color hierarchy. I shall look into the mirror and happily embrace the beautiful shade of yellow that I am. I am who I am, and no one can take that away from me.

SHE WANTS TO BE LIGHTER by Charmaine Tuason

When I was a little girl, the way that skin color was explained to me was in the story about three gingerbread men. The reason one gingerbread man was light was because the baker had taken him out of the oven too early. The reason the other gingerbread was dark was because the baker had taken him out of the oven much too late. Then there was one gingerbread man left . . . a sort of medium golden color . . . he was just right because the baker had taken him out just in time. I never gave this story much significance when I was a kid, but now I look back and realize how this simple gingerbread story has manifested itself in such a complex way in my own life story.

Much like the gingerbread men, I had been labeled light, medium, and dark. A meaning was also attached to each label: right, not quite right, and wrong. I wanted to believe that these labels had no affect on me. However, as part of the research team on Asian American colorism, I recognized a quiet pain and denial in my interviewees. I could only conclude that I was going through the same exact thing. In the process of writing this autobiography, I have had to quiet my inner voice, which has vehemently denied that colorism has had an impact on me and try to find the truth, the truth that I have been affected in some deep way.

An event that got me to start thinking about colorism in my culture was in high school. My boyfriend Mike and I were hanging out in his game room. He had been staring at a senior graduation picture of me that he had hung on his wall. "You look good with light skin, you should never try to get dark," he told me. I did not know what to say. I mean, how did he know whether I looked good light or dark . . . was not that a Filipino thing? *All right, who was the leak that told this White boy the unspoken rules?* Someone must have pulled him into some secret town meeting while my back was turned. Great! It was not enough for him to know how to eat adobo and learn a few basic words in Tagalog, but he just had to learn that Filipino girls look better with light skin. I did not get mad or frustrated, because I was not exactly sure whether or not I should be. I knew he was giving me a compliment but somehow, somewhere deep down inside, I felt like there was something strange about this compliment. Nevertheless, I took note. I suppose I took note because his opinion mattered to me at the time. What girl did not want to be beautiful and attractive to her boyfriend? Although the relationship ended years ago, his words stayed with me like a record playing over and over in my mind. Only in retrospect can I recognize that I had unconsciously made a pact . . . *okay, I'll try to stay light.* From that experience I had learned that I was the most attractive with light skin. *Light* meant *right*.

When I went off to college, I started dating Brian, a Filipino boy, who surprised me by declaring that I was not in fact light but medium in color. One day over lunch, Brian turned to me and asked if I thought he seemed darker today. I shrugged and answered that I had not noticed any difference. He stuck his arm out to the light and frowned at his own conclusions. His roommate Dante was sitting across from us.

> "What do you think, Dante?" Brian asked with a desperate look on his face.
> "I guess you look typical," Dante jokingly replied.
> Brian looked a little traumatized. "You don't understand because you're light skinned."

Dante just sat there in silent agreement. I was annoyed that he did not say anything to make Brian feel better so I thought I would give it a try.

> "Look, I'm light, but I totally understand."

They both burst into laughter. I was confused and suddenly self-conscious.

"You're not light!" Brian shouted in disbelief while studying my face for some sign that I was only joking. I was shocked. I began to mentally retrace my steps. *What happened between the time that Mike said I was light and when Brian said that I was medium?* I asked myself. Well, one answer was obvious. During my relationship with Mike, I had been living in Iceland, the coldest place on earth, where every inch of my skin was covered daily in a reflective parka. Now that I was with Brian, I was living in the sunniest and most skin-baring place on the face of the planet, Santa Barbara, California. When most people where thanking their lucky stars for living in such a beautiful city, I was thinking *Damn! Somebody get me outta here. I'm burning up!* Then I started to point fingers. Perhaps the reason was because the Filipinos in this school had more Chinese and Spanish blood than I did. I was starting to resent the fact that my mother's side of the family was dark. Why did God not bless us with lighter ancestry? How could I possibly compete with my lighter peers?

I was beginning to take colorism more seriously than before, because unlike Mike, Brian was Filipino. Brian knew the unspoken rules; he knew what he was saying. I started to think back to remarks that older Filipino friends and relatives would say about light and dark Filipinos. I had dismissed their remarks as old fashioned, but now I was realizing that skin color mattered to Filipino kids who were my age. I was taking note of this experience. Brian had called me medium, and I was beginning to unconsciously rate myself as second best. I was just thankful that I was not *dark*. I had obviously done a horrible job at maintaining my light color, so now that I was medium there was no way that I was ever going to let myself get *dark*. As a result, I found myself making the most ridiculous choices in my daily life.

In 2000, I enrolled in university summer classes. During one of the weekends, my roommates decided to ditch their reading and spend a day on the beach. They tried everything to get me to go, but I just did not want to get dark. Finally, I joined them, but insisted that I go in my jeans and in a long-sleeved shirt. Two hours later, my fair-skinned Caucasian roommates were nicely browned, all lined up on their bright beach towels. I was at the other end; my hair was completely soaked in sweat and my dark jeans were sticking to my skin. I looked as if I had jumped into a pool with all my clothes on. The most humiliating part was walking home in that state. I was just glad that I had survived the day without getting dark. I did not know what I would do if someone ever called me that unforgivable label.

Then two years later, it happened. A friend of my mother's called me a "dark beauty." I was so offended. "*Dark*" was a loaded word, and she pulled the trigger. She might as well have slapped an apron on me and called me the maid. The word *dark* and *beauty* just did not go together. Dark cancelled beauty out. Dark meant you were lower class, ugly, and unimportant. I found myself retracing steps once again. Now how did I manage to get from medium to dark? I could think of only one person—Sunitha.

Sunitha had been my roommate and an amazing influence. She was a beautiful and intelligent Asian Indian woman who took pride in being dark. In fact, she had a painting of a skin lightener that she hung on our wall to remind us all of the ridiculousness of skin lightening. The fear of getting dark had no hold over her, because she had made her choice and she was firmly standing her ground. Her carefree attitude eventually rubbed off on me, and I found myself doing things I never would have done ordinarily, like taking daily jogs on the beach or simply chilling under the sun. So, I knew exactly how and why I had become a "dark beauty." It never occurred to me that dark and beauty could coexist, although it was obviously clear through Sunitha that it could. I was just so distracted with the ideas and stereotypes of dark skin that I did not pay much attention to dark skin that was on real people, who could disprove dark stereotypes any day. The illusion was so great that I could not separate fact from fiction.

With no Sunitha to remind me, I started to feel self-conscious. Suddenly, those compliments that I had collected in my mind for years were resurfacing all at once to haunt me and taunt me. I desperately needed to be lighter, so I turned to the unthinkable—skin lightening. My mother and I went to the local Filipino store to buy a bottle. I paced back and forth through the aisle, not because I was indecisive about which brand, but because I was more embarrassed. I felt like I needed to apologize to somebody about my skin color, as if it was a burden for people to see. I also felt like the act of picking up the bottle and taking it to the register was some sort announcement to the world that I had given in. My mom had finished picking up a few things and was getting really impatient with me. "Just pick one!" she yelled from across the tiny store. I finally brought one up to the register. "She wants to be lighter," my mom announced to the clerk. The clerk did not seem to mind; she acted like it was the most natural thing in the world. But somehow I felt like I was losing some kind of test, one of those tests that check to see what kind of person you are when no one is looking, a test of integrity.

The lightener did not last a week. The idea of my skin slowly peeling away to the bone and wrinkling up like a raisin did not quite appeal to me. I was also feeling terribly guilty for not being as strong as Sunitha. I had crossed an invisible line into obsession, and I needed to find my way back home. I had had enough of this label telling me who I am and how I should be. The term *darkness* was questioning my intelligence, my beauty, and my worth. I knew I was a strong, beautiful, and intelligent woman; I had the friends, family, and education to prove it. Then in 2003, I had the opportunity to come face to face with these labels.

A college professor of mine gave me the option of writing a research paper on anything concerning Asian Americans. I chose to tackle colorism. Through my writing process, I found the unexpected: healing. The hypnotic power that color classification had on me was slowly wearing off. I also gained power over it, because I could recognize it in its most powerful form: the form of people I love and respect. When a *dark* baby cousin was born into my family a few months ago, I was constantly hearing remarks like, "Oh no, he took after his father's side of the family," or "It's okay to be a boy and be dark. Thank goodness he's not a girl." I held my cousin in my arms, inspecting his dark flesh and smiling, because I would be there and my work would be there to counter those voices. This baby was becoming a symbol of my hope that the work I had done and continue to do in the area of colorism would help him and others to develop a better concept of self and to be proud of whatever color their skin turns out to be.

COLORISM by Marybeth Liu

I am a five-foot-two-inch, twenty-one-year-old Asian American woman. I am a mix of Chinese and French. However, I identify myself as Chinese because I look more Asian, and I was only in touch with my Chinese culture throughout my entire life. My father is full-blooded Chinese, and my mother is three-fourths Chinese and hardly ever speaks of her one-fourth French side.

I grew up most of my life in Garden Grove, California. The neighborhood and its surrounding community hold a major Asian population. It was difficult growing up with a mixed ethnic background because I was not always accepted. I recall at a young age that my mother and father attempted to cover up my mixed appearance by sending me to Chinese school, so that I would act really Chinese, dressing me up "Asian," and drilling Asian culture into me. I never really understood why it was so important to look and act Asian.

It was when I was in the fourth grade that I realized why my parents tried so hard to hide my true identity. I was sitting on the swings when an Asian girl came up to me and asked me what ethnicity I was. I replied that I am Chinese American. Kids being kids, she said I did not look pure Asian and that I looked funny. She ran off, and I was left confused and hurt. The following day at school, I noticed my peers were laughing and whispering in my presence. I thought it was how I was dressed or maybe I had something on my face. I decided to just ignore my surroundings and concentrate on the teacher. That day at recess, the same little girl approached me and said she saw my parents drop me off at school that morning and she noticed they looked Asian. I stated that they are Asian, so she responded with, "Were you adopted?" At this point I was irritated, and I asked her why she had to be so rude. She looked at me with her dark brown eyes and said, "Because you are different from me and everyone else in the class." She pointed out that my hair was a curly brown with some red in it, my eyes were not dark like hers, I had freckles, and my skin was not pale but white. It was from this day on that colorism affected my life, because up until the sixth grade, I never had friends; no one wanted to be friends with the girl that was different.

The following year I started junior high. I decided to commute to a junior high school in Santa Ana, thirty minutes away from where I lived. I wanted to get away from all the gossip about me being adopted or my mother having an affair with a White man and from feeling so secluded. The summer before I began junior high, I straightened my hair, dyed it jet black, wore glasses to hide my lighter eyes, wore foundation in an attempt to hide my freckles, and tried to tan my white skin. It was definitely successful, because I was able to pass myself off as an Asian all through junior high with absolutely no one ever questioning my ethnic authenticity. There were occasions when someone would comment that I had lighter eyes than most Asians, but that was about it.

I also attended high school in Santa Ana. My high school was made up mainly of Asians, with a few Whites and Hispanics. The trend with Asians was to lighten their hair, give it highlights, and try to look "more American." By the end of my freshman year, I decided I would let my natural appearance come out, because looking "more American" was the trend. So when summer came, I stopped dying my hair and let it grow to its natural color. I stopped wearing foundation, and I got contacts. And then I had the shock of my life. The first day of fall I stepped onto campus for my sophomore year. Everyone I knew and anyone who normally recognized me with dark hair and glasses had eyes larger than a bowling ball. Some did not approach me but stood and stared. My friends asked me, "What the heck happened to you? How come you changed so much over the summer?" I said, "This is what I really look like." They had a hard time believing me, because ever since junior high, I had looked so Asian. Some of my friends would not have anything to do with me, although others did not act any different. I could not understand what the big deal was. I was just trying to look like the trend, the "American" look—which is what I really looked like!

I went home crying to my parents after the school day ended. This was the first and only time we ever spoke of my mixed heritage. My mother did not like to talk about it, because it was not a happy story. All I know is that my grandmother was kidnapped by a French soldier and forced to marry him. Throughout our conversation, my mother refused to answer my questions regarding my European heritage. Her reply was, "Both your parents are Chinese and that is all we know how to practice." I told them that people at school see and know I am not full-blood Chinese, so they do not accept me as only Chinese. My mother's response was simply, "Your real friends will accept you for who you are." My father was more reassuring. He commented that the Asian community in which we lived was not all completely open-minded about multiracial individuals yet but that they would be in time. Although my dad's comment made me feel a bit better, I still wanted to know why people treated me like I was from Mars and how I could be more accepted by the Asian community. My parents then asked me why I personally felt it was so important to be accepted by people and to be classified as Asian. I replied that everyone around me seemed to know where they belonged, and I wanted to belong somewhere, too. If I identified myself as Chinese, people should accept it and not categorize me differently based on my physical features.

Later that night, I had a private conversation with my mother. I asked her why she looked so upset when we discussed our mixed-race background. She hesitated a moment and finally replied that when she was growing up in China, people would ignore her or sometimes even spit on her because she was different. She admitted that she chose to marry my father so that her children would look more Asian, and so they would not have to go through all that she did. I told my mother that it was hard, but I would never trade my heritage, because I am who I am. It was bizarre—I came to the realization by talking to my mother that I really did not care any longer what anyone thought of me and my appearance. I went on through high school, and whenever anyone asked about my unusual appearance, I stated that I was of mixed ancestry but that my culture was full-blooded Chinese.

My parents told me not too long ago that they were hoping my short height, small feet, petite frame, and short eyelashes, plus their drilling Chinese culture into me, would help me pass for "pure" Asian. I asked them the same question they had asked me years earlier: Why they felt that it was such a big deal to be identified as Asian. They commented that, when they first came to America, everything was so unfamiliar. They wanted to live in a community where there were people who had similar experiences to theirs and where they would be accepted. However, the Asian community in the early 1980s was not quick to accept multiracial individuals, so they had to cover up any trace of my mother's European ancestry to fit securely into, and receive support from, the Asian American community.

I guess we all have our reasons for wanting to identify with a specific group. I feel it is quite unfortunate that I never got to learn about my European heritage because of my parents' fear of other people's ignorance. Recently, I have been attempting to learn about my European ancestors through my mother and her sisters, but they are still in denial themselves about their multiracial heritage. I believe they are still in hiding because of the difficult experiences they had growing up as multiracial people in China. I, too, fear that I will not be accepted by people as Asian—or even accepted by them as a person—because I am of mixed heritage. But my fear has lessened over the years because I keep in mind that times have changed; there are a lot more people like me these days, and people are more open-minded. Moreover, I have come to realize that if I choose to identity myself as an Asian and someone else may not agree, I really do not care very much what they think. I am mature enough to know that an outsider can have their opinion of where I should be categorized, but the only thing that really matters is how I am most comfortable identifying myself.

In summary, my parents never really discussed colorism with me. They just taught me the Chinese culture and let me define my relationship to my color and features myself. What I admire most about my parents is that I have never heard them judge or stereotype anyone. Even when I was going through my identity crisis, they never commented on Asians or White Americans. Their response was always "It will get better with time, and remember to see people from their heart." Who cares what color your skin, hair, or eyes are? These are only physical characteristics. The way I see it, when we die, who is going to remember us for our race or ethnicity? Realistically, people will remember us for how we affected them in their lives and for what each of us has accomplished as an individual. We ought to be able to ignore people's physical characteristics and society's stereotypes of ethnic groups and races. We are all one and the same.

"YOU HAVE THE MOST BEAUTIFUL SKIN COLOR!"
by Sara Cruz

"You have the most beautiful skin color!" "I love your hair!" "Are your lips real?" I have heard these phrases throughout my life and have learned almost to expect them. Growing up as an Asian American in a mainly White neighborhood and society, I was repeatedly pointed out as having specific features and characteristics that people found unusual and attractive. Because my social environment was mostly White, my dark skin, brown hair, and large lips definitely stuck out in a crowd. But while I can say that my phenotypical features stood out, I cannot say they were not accepted. People I met usually commented on how much they liked my features. Yet while most people were attracted to the way I look, I often believe that it was simply because I am half Asian and half White, and my combined heritage intrigued them.

My dark skin is almost always pointed out as my biggest physical blessing. My father's dark Filipino skin mixed with my Polish mother's extremely fair skin has given me a shade somewhere in the middle. White people I have known have always liked my skin because it reminds them of healthy, tan skin. So while it is socially more acceptable to be a White person than to be Asian or anything else, it seems to be attractive in pop culture to have a darker, tanner shade of White people's skin. Because of my darker skin and mixed background, I am found to be physically acceptable and attractive as an Asian American in a White environment. Being blessed with my father's dark, full hair has also been admired by Whites. While the saying is that "blondes have more fun," my long brown hair gave me a distinctive, exotic appearance. My grandparents from Hawai'i also insisted on sending me little flower clips and barrettes to put in my hair. With these additions, I looked even more exotic and even a bit Hawaiian. So while I was not White, having an exotic island look worked in my favor—being Hawaiian is in style.

Being a Hapa in a White community has given me a physical advantage over monoracial people in my society, in that I am able to blend in and be accepted because my mixed features are found different and intriguing. While I have learned to love my distinctive characteristics, I did not always feel this way. I was often teased for having such a flat nose while most of the other White students had sharp, straight ones. My full lips were the topic of conversation and ridicule so often that I made up stories saying I hit my lips on something and that's why they looked so big. But while these features are frequently pointed out and sometimes criticized in the White community, the Asian community has not always proven to be a more suitable place for my distinctive features.

While my dark skin was often seen as a virtue by the White community, it was a differentiating factor between myself and monoracial Asian Americans. In the Asian community I was familiar with, which was made up largely of Chinese and Japanese people, fair skin was preferred above my dark Filipino skin. Because my dark skin is such a large distinctive physical feature, it has sometimes been a separating trait between me and most of the Asian American majority. This type of attitude was much different from the acceptance I generally received from the White community concerning my skin shade.

My eyes have also been a large difference between me and the monoracial Asian American community. My mixed heritage resulted in having my mother's round eyes with her European double eyelids. Because I did not inherit my father's almond-shaped eyes, with smooth eyelids, I look different from other Asian Americans. But instead of seeing this difference as being a negative aspect, I have found in many past experiences that my eye shape is actually envied by many of my Asian American peers. In fact, while most teenagers attempt breast enhancement surgery and even liposuction, many of my Asian American friends opted for eyelid surgery. The plastic surgery artificially provides the patient with double eyelids like those of White people. While this intense surgery may seem strange, I have found that European eyes are preferred over the usual Asian eye shape, at least among Asian Americans my age.

Being mixed, I have experienced different reactions to my skin color and features from different groups. Maybe that difference is the only constant thing: How I am viewed, and to a certain extent how I feel about myself, depends on who is doing the viewing.

TANGENT ROAD: FROM A FIRST GENERATION NOYBIAN PERSPECTIVE by Luz Devadason

Racism is supposed to be a thing of the past. Nobody likes to hear the word *racism*. It has that nails-against-the-chalkboard sound to it. For some it sounds like useless whining. To others the oppression is an inescapable reality. With that said, let's talk about it.

I am an American mixed woman of color. I would like to think of my experience as unique, but the more I talk to people of mixed ancestry and read ethnic studies autobiographies, the more I find out how we are the same. It shocked me to realize that my life seemed to run parallel with so many others purely based on our ethnic makeup. How could this be? I was raised to believe everyone is their own individual regardless of race or gender, but the more I learned, the more I came to understand how society judges and categorizes, making our experiences coincide.

I did an informal field study on my life for three months and found out on average I get asked, "What are you?" about twenty times a week. One day on a movie set, I got asked fifty-two times. It's not *what* I am that determines how I am treated. It is *how* I am viewed. It's those life experiences of a person of color that bond those minority communities together. That makes me ethnically identify with almost every person-of-color community. Those who disagree may not come from such a chameleon of a background, and that is their privilege: to be able to put themselves into a neat little box with a check and expect the same from others. I cannot and will not do that. I know that I have colonial blood in me, but I have never been viewed as "White." Does my blood override my experience?

Let's face it. The terms "American" and "White" are used synonymously by most Americans. If this was not so, I don't know why I get asked what my nationality is all the time. When I reply, "I'm American," I get, "But where were you from originally?" As if I can not be part of this country because I am Brown. When I tell them "Connecticut," this frustrates them. Their reply is, "But where were you born?" I was born in Connecticut (a state in the United States of America), I speak English without an accent (maybe a California one, because for most of my life I have lived out here), I wear jeans and tank tops, and I love watching TV and eating pepperoni and mushroom pizza with the occasional beer. I am American. It's just that I cannot be viewed as such because I'm not White. My appearance to many people is foreign—exotic. This makes them think I am Un-American.

I wonder how I can finish writing this without getting into my heritage that I'm proud of. I have had Latina girls tell me that my choice not to identify meant I was ashamed of my background. This hurt me. I love my parents dearly, but my choice to not check off a box other than "other" is to prove that not being able to racially classify someone can be uncomfortable because we are raised to categorize. I told the girls that my hair color was natural and my eyes were really brown. I was not ashamed of what my parents gave me. I do not hide behind colored contacts. One of the girls had fake green eyes and blond hair with her black roots showing. I don't blame her for this. It's hard when your parents don't want you to speak Spanish at school, hang out with Mexican boys, or be out in the sun too long.

I have dated a few Asian Americans. The issue of my skin tone being too dark has been a problem in almost all of my relationships. All of a sudden I am Black, I am Mexican, I am Indian, I am everything that is not Asian to them. It's not just the displacement of my ethnic identity that bothers me. It's that the idea of being all those "other things" makes me ugly to their families. I have had to wait in the car while my boyfriend I lived with had to get things from his parents' house, because his mother did not want a "Black" girl in her home. It makes me so frustrated, because family acceptance is important to me. I am close to my family, and I can't imagine a life when I wouldn't be close to my husband's family. What type of life would that be for my children? With Latino families this is not the case as much, because I can speak some Spanish. The cultural ties outweigh my mixed blood. That and my skin tone is not as big of an issue because I phenotypically fit in more with Latinos than I do with Asians (except for the Filipino and some Southeast Asian communities). Multiracial people generally are accepting.

I understand the Asian culture and their respect for elders in the family. I never expected any one of these men to tell their families that I was beautiful as a dark woman and that their families would have to deal with their own bigotry. Although as I write this, I realize that maybe in the back of my head I really did wish for it. These men were not cowards but felt that to explain this to elders would be disrespectful, because they were already old and set in their ways. What was the point if they didn't care what their family thought anyway? One man attempted to discuss the racism his grandmother felt toward me after I had a long cry on his shoulder, and I still love him for it. Whether the outcome was any different, I don't know. I do know that I spent many a night wishing his grandmother could dislike me for something I could actually control.

From a completely Western perspective, this may seem odd. Love is supposed to conquer all. I have lived in America my whole life. I find myself conflicted in what I expect in relationships with different cultural values tugging at me. Both of my parents are first-generation immigrants. Their experiences are so vastly different from my own and from one another that I have learned to be empathetic to different cultural perspectives. I know that both of my parents did not get to pass on as much of their heritage as they could have if they married someone mixed with their background. This makes me understand why first-generation parents or grandparents feel wary about their sons bringing me home. They just don't want to lose a significant part of their family's culture and heritage. Understanding doesn't make it any easier, but it's still good to know.

In the Black community, being mixed is more common. I am no longer too dark. However, I get hated on by darker Black women who feel I am not Black enough, or maybe they secretly envy me because of programmed self-hate. When people try to guess my background, they dissect me. My nose is broader, my lips are full, and my butt is too big for a Korean. Therefore, I must be part African. My hair isn't kinky but that can be explained by my mixed ancestry or maybe that my hair is a weave. As I write, my hair is in braids. Although I'm initially accepted in the Black community, I am called a Puerto Rican mami, Asian cutie, or island girl. I'm everything that is not Black, minus the community with social consciousness. They proudly claim me as another sista.

The lady who braids my hair said she could tell I was mixed when she first spoke with me on the phone. I guess I don't talk ghetto enough at times. I sound educated. Does that mean being educated means not being Black? She was happy that I was aware of the community's problems and gladly took me in. On pulling at my hair to throw some braids in she came to the conclusion that I was Korean and Black. Usually I don't take the time to explain myself for various reasons. Sometimes it makes me sad; sometimes it makes me feel like I'm in a petri dish; sometimes I'm just sick of it; sometimes it turns into having to defend myself, but most of the time I know they won't get it. I hope as you read this, you are getting it.

If there are so many problems with dating people of color, why don't I hook up with a White guy? Despite the prejudice within people-of-color communities, in my experience, I find it harder to date White people. When I dated White guys I was exotic. It was like they were trying something new, or I felt like I was a fetish because his "last few girlfriends were Asian," or "Mexican," or "Hawaiian." Even White liberal guys could not stop making comments about how I fit some stereotype. Even my White girlfriends tell me I'm lucky to be so mixed and full of culture. They wish they "had a culture instead of being just White." But they do have a culture, even if nobody asks them where they were from. Their ancestry is still from somewhere. I guess it is harder to want to learn about your roots when you don't have to be constantly reminded of them.

Despite all of our efforts to be in touch with our roots, so many sisters and brothers in people-of-color communities hide their brown eyes behind colored contacts. A dark Black girlfriend of mine said she felt ugly without her blue contacts. Her self-esteem was affected by her real brown eyes. When people of color conform to White beauty we physically change ourselves, usually permanently: our eyes, our hair, our bleach soap that strips the pigment of who we are and where we came from. Many people of color marry White people because they are thought to be more attractive, giving them a "raised" societal status and their children a higher chance of passing off into the White world of beauty. Internalized self-hate is powerful conditioning. I can't make my dark Black girlfriend feel beautiful without her blue contacts. I have tried. She has to start accepting herself first.

White kids rarely, if ever, wear brown contacts. They will not dye their hair unless they are Goth or artsy. They will go to tanning salons—but not to be Brown and definitely not to look Black. White people get to embrace a "different" culture by putting on a shirt or dress that they can take off at the end of the day. It is something *on* their bodies, not *in* their bodies or minds. No one asks them *what* they are, because they are so used to being asked *who* they are. No one expects them to change *who* they are, and no one forces them to choose between their identities. Those who are brave enough to recognize racism still cannot disassociate from the privileges that they are allowed to take for granted.

I used to go-go dance at a club in Santa Barbara. The club did not want to attract Mexicans and Blacks anymore, so they decided to stop playing hip hop and got rid of me. I was disappointed, but not surprised. It is a rich White town. I moved to L.A. where I danced at a Salsa club. I learned to always answer I was half of whatever ethnic background they asked about. This carried into other jobs. When I started acting I would always get asked in my audition what I was. All roles are ethnically specified. There is a reason why there are more White people on TV. It's probably because people of color were not allowed to try out to be a "Friend," or live in "90210." Can you imagine how much it sucked to truly realize that this idea of race not only influenced my love life but was going to determine whether I could feed myself? In addition to having to be boxed into an ethnicity when I auditioned, across the board it was usually to play a maid, prostitute, gang banger's girlfriend, video ho, some druggie, or a girl in a threesome. Our media projects women-of-color as third-class citizens. I have been half-Chumash, half-Latina, full Puerto Rican, half-Vietnamese, full Filipina, half-Black, half-Hawaiian, half-Indian, full Cambodian, half-whatever-they-needed-me-to-be, because they thought I already was. Those dreaded boxes again.

So many boxes to check, yet none of them I could fit into. There hasn't been a box society has created for me yet, and I refuse to compromise my experience to appease anyone. Because we *have* to check off a box society creates for us, I might as well cave in and tell you what multiracial box I'm in. I'm Noybian. Let me tell you about my people's history.

Noybians are from the small island of Noybia that used to exist in the Mediterranean Sea thousands of years ago before the continents broke up. The people were mixed from surrounding countries from Asia, Africa, and Europe. These people were dreamers who were about acceptance and freedom. Noybians welcomed all people who shared the same spirit. Because there was no segregation according to physical appearances, Noybians have always been from a rich cultural background.

The island provided good homes from the dark woods and plentiful nourishment from the fruit that hung a few feet from the ground. The ocean was full of fish, and the air was warm with gentle breezes. The universal language was Noybianese, though it is said that the main influences of the dialect were derived from ancient Egypt. It is no wonder, because many of the first peoples of earth are from Mesopotamia. Noybians' history is vague because they did not have a written text. Like griots from Africa, history was passed orally from one generation to the next. There is no one alive today who speaks Noybianese.

Sadly, as time passed, traders came on this small island. What was once a haven became someone else's dollar sign. People did not know how to categorize Noybians. Although the Noybians had European ancestry from Spain, Greece, and France, Europeans decided to call them savages. What was known as the one-drop rule hundreds of years later came to pass on the Noybians. The majority of Noybians were brought into slavery and died quickly, because a dreamer spirit cannot be caged. Others grew sick with the disease spawned from colonial power and died from trying to save the only place in the world they could have existed. Because history is only written by the winners, the island of Noybia is now said never to have existed. Nobody wants to take responsibility for the destruction of an entire group of people and way of life shared. To this day, nobody knows which island was Noybia or if the island is even above water anymore.

Noybians could only have lived in a time where racial classification did not exist. As soon as the social construct of race emerged to dehumanize fellow brothers and sisters, there was no place in the world for people like Noybians. My ancestry is Noybian. I am proud of my background. It was not easy to get here, but it is where I am at.

I have shared my mixed-heritage experience with others who are mixed with all sorts of different ethnicities. The sentiments were the same. The frustrations were similar, and now we have come full circle to what I have been saying all along. It is how people view you that determines how you are treated. My mixed friends and I do not have the same blood mix, but because our experience is so much the same, it bonds us together. We are a multiracial community within ourselves. A lot of my friends of mixed heritage identify as NOYBian. **N**one **O**f **Y**our **B**usiness. It's because it is the only category we feel like we can be in without having to deal with not being enough or conforming to preexisting implications. Noybia was created. Race was created. If I have to classify myself under a socially constructed term, I would rather it be under my own.

WHAT DO YOU FEEL MORE? by Karen Jackson

I never knew the terms "interracial," "biracial" or "Eurasian" until I reached junior high school, and even then they were just words to me, not something I learned to embrace till much later on. My parents never sat me aside and said, "Mommy is Sansei Japanese American and Daddy is Caucasian American with his ancestors from Germany, England and Ireland, and we got married despite our racial and religious differences. You will never have to choose one race over the other, you are both Japanese and Caucasian and even though you may struggle with your racial identity, you should never feel like you have to choose one or the other, because you are both."

Yeah, right. This was the 1980s in Sunnyvale, not the 2020s where everyone most likely will be half this, half that, and probably half of that. But what I did know was that when my brother and I had our "My bologna has a first name, it's O-S-C-A-R. My bologna has a second name it's M-A-Y-E-R" hot dogs with our mac 'n' cheese, Mom would make sukiyaki with the same O-S-C-A-R M-A-Y-E-Rs. I knew that in preschool when I drew a picture of my family, I needed the black, brown, *and* yellow Crayola markers. I knew that after Mom and I finished shopping at the supermarket that we would go to Mr. Imahara's store to buy fruit and vegetables, because Mom said, "they just don't know how to grow fruit at the normal grocery store." And I knew that it was just a regular summer to go to bible study while visiting my grandparents in Orange County one week and then go to the Obon festival at the Buddhist temple the next.

I would play with my Strawberry Shortcake and Hello Kitty dolls the same. I would pick the dolls with dark hair and dark eyes before any others. J-town was a treat for me. I collected origami paper. I had the same pencil cases from Sanrio as the other Japanese girls, and we would compete for who had the best ones with the most features. When I got the Hello Kitty one that you could press buttons, and the pencil sharpener would pop out along with the magnifying glass, that was it, I was in. We would pay "*ichi, ni, san*" on the tan barked playground, a Japanese version of "paper, rock, scissors." Grandpa Hiromoto would always give us dried fruit when we would visit.

I joined the Girl Scouts when I was six years old. I loved going to baseball games with my grandfather as a child and eating hot dogs and malts. My mom would pack me lunches with peanut butter sandwiches and pudding cups. I wore Oshkosh clothes. I played with Cabbage Patch Kids. Grandmommie Jackson would always give us Cocoa Puffs and Strawberry Quik when we would visit. This was just what a "normal" childhood was like for me, and I didn't see much wrong with it.

Despite the occasional "Chinese, Japanese, Korean, American!" taunting on the playground with the squishing, pulling, and tugging of the eyes, my first racial identity crisis occurred during third grade SRA testing. It began the same as any annual SRA test. The teacher explained that we would all be tested but that it was nothing to worry about. We followed the teacher in a single file as we dragged our Velcro Stride Rites across the blacktop to the multipurpose room. It always felt weird having assemblies, watching performances, and eating my tater tots in the same place.

I sat down and instantly grabbed the freshly sharpened number two pencil. "Everyone put down your pencils and keep your hands in your laps," my teacher's voice boomed across the room. Oops. "First fill in your name and do not open the test booklet until I say so. Please write neatly and fill in the bubbles completely. Do not write outside of the bubbles. Remember how I showed you? In circles," as she drew a tiny circle with her index finger in the air.

I began filling out the form. Last name, J-A-C . . . ensuring that my bubbles were filled in completely. First name, done. Grade, done. Teacher, done. Race/Ethnicity? I paused. *Fill in one bubble only: Caucasian/Non-Hispanic, Black/African-American, Hispanic/Latino, Asian Pacific Islander, or Native American.* What the hell do you mean one bubble only? Mom's Japanese and Dad's Caucasian. Now what was I supposed to do? It clearly stated that I could fill in one bubble only, so now what? I reached down to my shoe and pulled the Velcro up, down, up, down. Zitch-Zitch. Zitch-Zitch. Too many questions filled my ten-year-old mind. Should I ask the teacher what to do? Will the other kids laugh at me? It should be a simple question. Why can I not just answer it?

My hand shot up in the air.

"Yes Karen, what is it?" the teacher's irritated voice snapped at me.

"I have a question. What do I put for Race/Ethnicity?"

"What do you mean?"

"Well, my mom is Japanese, and my dad is, uh, not. What do I put if I can't fill in two bubbles?"

"What do you feel more?"

Now this stumped me. What do I feel more? What is she talking about? *Feel more*? How can I feel more of one thing than the other? If I chose Asian/Pacific Islander, would that be betraying Dad? What if I chose Caucasian/Non-Hispanic? Would it mean that I loved one more than the other?

"What do you mean *feel more*?"

Silence.

My mind began racing. I am White. I am Asian. Yes, my last name is Jackson. Yes, I have light skin. Yes, I have brown hair and not black like my brother's. Does that make him more Asian than I am because he has darker hair? Dad has darker hair than me, and that doesn't make him Asian, so that logic just doesn't work. Most Asians are short, and I am short. Does that make me more Asian? But then again, I had Dad's feet. But, come to think of it, I had Mom's hands. I get sunburned easily, and it is hard for me to get a tan. Does that make me more Caucasian? I choose jasmine rice over rice pilaf any day of the week. Does that make me more Asian?

"Well," she stammered, "You look more White. So just fill in the bubble that says Caucasian/Non-Hispanic."

Sorry Mommy.

As I grew older I found myself to have nothing in common with the other Caucasian students. Because I am White and all, I will just call them White. The other White kids in school would always get paid for their grades: $5 for each *A* or for some $20 for each *A*. When I asked my mom one time why I didn't get paid for my grades, she replied, "You don't get paid for your grades because you are expected to get good grades. You should never be rewarded for something that you are expected to do." End of conversation.

They were the first ones to get a phone in their room, even their own lines by the age of twelve, and get to talk on their light-up phones as late as they wanted each night. Their parents would bring them McDonald's at lunch time, as the rest of us were eating our chimichangas and half-frozen apple juice. They would be spoiled with the latest clothes, toys, and candy despite talking back to their parents and calling them nasty names. How could I possibly relate to that? No way would my Mom ever allow me to eat that sort of junk for lunch, let alone talk back to her. I couldn't even *think* about talking back to her as I was convinced that she could read my mind even before thinking about it. Just the way it was: no ifs, ands, or buts about it.

In junior high, it started to become popular to be Asian, Black, or La-tino—well, basically as long as you were ethnic anything, you would be all right. Of course, there were some ethnicities that were seen as cooler than others. If you were Black, Latino, or Filipino you were considered the coolest. Then those who were mixed or passed as Black, Latino, or Filipino, and the occasional White girl who could hairspray her hair in the perfect wave and grew up in the projects who had her *get-out-of-jail-free* card.

The Korean, Chinese, and Japanese kids usually stuck together. They had curfews, had first-generation parents, and could invite their friends over and not be embarrassed of grandma who lived with them or the strange Chi-nese smells coming from the kitchen. It became apparent who was what, who belonged where, and who didn't belong. It was not always about who was a jock, a nerd, a skater, a gangster, or any other style or hobby-driven category. Looks and color became the deciding factor as to your "coolness" on the social scale and your worth.

In high school, maybe I was a wannabe Asian, because it just was not seen as cool to be White. White people had no rhythm. White people thought they were better than everyone else. White people were bland and were just the non-flavored uninteresting ones. They were the skaters, the punks, the headbangers, the anarchists, the preppies, the jocks, the cheerleaders, the nerds, the geeks, the weird drama students, or the band geeks. They just were not down with the OPP, ABC, or BBD, but they liked AC/DC. They didn't know what it was like to be from the other side of the tracks, and they didn't stand in line every month to get a free bus pass. They didn't eat lunch in the cafeteria, let alone get free meal tickets. On the other hand, they did get to miss school the morning of their sixteenth birthday to take their driving test and came home to a fixed-up 1969 red Mustang that their daddy bought them. They did get into their first-, second- and even third-choice colleges and never had to worry about how they would pay for it, books, or the gallons of beer they would consume.

Despite constantly gravitating toward and feeling like I fit in with the Asian crowd, I had the problem that because I looked stereotypically Whiter than I felt, I had to constantly reaffirm my Asian-ness to be accepted. No hair dye or tanning salon could change my nose, my freckles, or long legs. It was as if I was not accepted where I felt I belonged. Being White became my handicap in so many situations, with even good friends justifying my Hapa identity to others with, "Nah, man, she's cool. She's not full White, she's only half," pushing the fact that I was only half and that it really was not my fault for looking the way that I do. Where would I fit into this mixture of identities? Where would I belong?

As I grew older the fill-in-the-bubble racial identification questions crossed my path more often as the six racial bubbles began to multiply. They came up with this category, *Other*. Does that really make it easier for those of us who are multiracial? I didn't understand why I had to pick *Other* in the first place. It made me feel like I was the last kid picked at dodge ball. In college entrance forms the categories turned into subcategories and then subcategories of those subcategories. Asian/Pacific Islander became: Chinese, Japanese, Korean, Filipino, Asian Indian, or Islander, and I still couldn't pick more than one. But you could pick the not-so-wonderful category, *Other*.

No doubt I have been called "White girl" as a racist remark or out of pure affection from friends and enemies in my day. I would never compare it to the racism that my ancestors or other Americans have endured in the past, but it did create a great deal of confusion growing up. I have been assaulted for not hanging out in "the right crowd" (code for not being Asian enough), and I have been commended for not "selling out" on my Asian-ness and "keeping it real." Perhaps others struggled with labeling me with a category that they felt comfortable with more so than I ever did. As in the real world, *Other* just didn't cut it.

I no longer have the black eyes (marble eyes as my grandfather would call them) or the strawberry blonde hair I had as a child, as my eyes have lightened to a chocolate brown and my hair has darkened without a trace of natural blonde left in it. I tend to darken my hair and to avoid psychoanalyzing it, I will admit that it is possible that I do it to reaffirm my Asian-ness to myself more than anything. My mom says I am lucky because I can dye my hair brown, red, or blonde and can still look "normal"—whatever that means.

Somewhere along the line, must have been during my college years, it became cool to be Hapa. Perhaps Keanu Reeves, Dean Cain, and Tiger Woods have paved the way for us all. My Asian male friends started to seek out the Hapa girls, looking beyond the Asian girls. Maybe it was because they were tired of traditional parents of their Asian female counterparts. I have been told that Hapa girls are better than Asian girls, because you get the best of both worlds. They are Asian enough to please your parents, but White enough so they don't look like your sister. They are the White girl you have always wanted to be with but with a touch of soy to give you something in common.

Recently I have heard my Asian male friends tell me how much they want a White girlfriend. They have moved beyond their Hapa girl phase and are into their White girl stage. Perhaps because we are getting older, they are starting to envision what their children will look like and want Hapa kids. White women to them were once untouchable, and I have actually read in a fashion magazine that it's the nouveaux thing for a White woman to have an Asian boyfriend, the latest accessory that every girl should have. Forget the Jimmy Choo shoes, give me Jimmy! But these Asian guys who look for the White girlfriend are often the same men who look down on Asian women who date White men. Can't really win, can you?

I have begun to accept the fact that I am Hapa and may not always fit into a category chosen by myself or others. I could pick one of the (though stereotypical) grouping of my own: egg, twinkie, half-breed, half-caste, mutt, Hapa, Mestiza, multiracial, mixed, half-and-half, combo, multicultural, or one of my favorites: Oriental Jackson. My grandfather told me once that he came to the realization that his family name is being brought down by a bunch of "Oriental Jacksons." He was not trying to be racist in any way; he just made a poor joke. With my father who married a Japanese American, and my brother married to a Vietnamese American, the next generation of Jacksons will be a new breed of Oriental Jacksons. Who would have thought immigrating from Europe hundreds of years ago would have changed the entire Jackson concept? I am sure my ancestors never did.

Racism, stereotypes, and categories in society translate into all cultures of the world, but those who can truly function in it will take the fluid approach and adapt an identity they are comfortable (or even not) within each particular situation. There will always be people who challenge you and the category you identify with along the way, at least certainly in my case. I know that more often than not I will not be offered chopsticks when I walk into an Asian restaurant and will be given a spoon and fork. To this day, my mom's comfort food is her O-S-C-A-R M-A-Y-E-R sukiyaki, while mine is mac 'n' cheese. Does that make me more American? Perhaps. Japanese food will always be my favorite food. Does that make me more Asian? Perhaps. I will never eat chicken feet at *dim sum*. Does that make me more White? Perhaps.

NOTES

1. Some of the names of contributors to this chapter are pseudonyms.

· *3* ·

The Survey[1]

METHOD

In 2003, a team of researchers, working out of the University of California, Santa Barbara, interviewed ninety-nine Asian Americans from various ethnic communities around the state. The people we interviewed were immigrants and people born in the United States, women and men. They ranged in age from sixteen to eighty-two (see appendix 2).

The researchers asked each person interviewed background demographic questions including their age, ethnicity, and generation in this country. Then they zeroed in on colorism, asking the respondents about what they have observed in their communities as well as their own preferences as to skin and eye color, face shape, and so on. The interviewers asked them whether they had witnessed teasing or discrimination for or against any Asian Americans on account of skin color or features. They asked the interviewees to assess their own skin color and the skin colors they would prefer for their spouses and children. The interviewers asked them to respond to pictures of three Asian American women who had different shades of skin (more about that in a later part of this chapter). The interviewers also estimated the skin color of each respondent. For a list of the questions that the interviewers asked, see appendix 1.

Table 3.1 shows the distribution of the respondents by ethnic group and age.

Table 3.2 shows the distribution of the respondents by ethnic group and generation. As is customary in the study of immigration, "first generation" refers to immigrants who came to the United States themselves. "Second generation" refers to their children; "third generation" to their grandchildren, and so on. In the last decade and a half, influenced by terminology used by

Table 3.1.   Interview Respondents by Ethnic Group and Age

Ethnic Group	16–25	26–39	40–59	60+	Total
Cambodian	4	0	0	0	4
Cambodian Chinese	8	2	0	0	10
Chinese	16	1	0	0	17
Filipino	8	5	6	8	27
Filipino Mixed	7	1	0	0	8
South Asian	2	0	0	0	2
Japanese	6	3	3	3	15
Korean	9	0	0	0	9
Vietnamese	5	0	0	0	5
Vietnamese Chinese	2	0	0	0	2
Total	67	12	9	11	99

observers of Korean American communities, "1.5 generation" refers to people who immigrated to the United States as young children. Technically they are first generation, for they are immigrants, but socially and culturally they are as close to the perceptual, attitudinal, and behavioral patterns of the second generation as they are to those of the first.[2]

Table 3.3 shows the distribution of the respondents by ethnic group and gender.

All those interviewed were asked more or less the same questions; this study is not quantitative social science. It is more like social observation. It is likely some social scientists will not be fully satisfied with the methods employed. They may argue that what they regard as the ground rules for social scientific investigation were not sufficiently followed. From the perspective of the interviewers, however, method is not about rules. It is about approaches.

Table 3.2.   Interview Respondents by Ethnic Group and Generation

Ethnic Group	First Generation	1.5 Generation	Second Generation	Third or Fourth Generation	Total
Cambodian	2	0	2	0	4
Cambodian Chinese	2	1	7	0	10
Chinese	4	1	10	2	17
Filipino	18	3	5	1	27
Filipino Mixed	1	1	3	3	8
South Asian	0	0	2	0	2
Japanese	4	0	5	6	15
Korean	0	2	7	0	9
Vietnamese	0	1	4	0	5
Vietnamese Chinese	0	0	2	0	2
Total	31	9	47	12	99

Table 3.3.   Interview Respondents by Ethnic Group and Gender

Ethnic Group	Women	Men	Total
Cambodian	4	0	4
Cambodian Chinese	8	2	10
Chinese	8	9	17
Filipino	18	9	27
Filipino Mixed	3	5	8
South Asian	2	0	2
Japanese	10	5	15
Korean	7	2	9
Vietnamese	3	2	5
Vietnamese Chinese	0	2	2
Total	63	36	99

The interviewers are trying to figure things out. They have identified a problem—or perhaps it will turn out to be a series of more-or-less related problems. The interviewers are trying to figure out what are the issues at work in the problem (or problems) of colorism, and they are trying to point in the directions of some interpretations.

It is a bit like slow journalism.[3] That is, the interviewers are questioning, investigating, observing, recording, reaching after meaning, and reporting—not in the rapid-fire manner of journalistic writing but with a bit more time for systematic investigation and reflection. The method is empirical, reflexive, and informed both by theory and by other empirical studies. But it is primarily wandering in a fog-shrouded new territory and trying to discern the shapes of things encountered there.[4] They are interested in truth—in learning how things are—not as if that were something objective and knowable but as a regulative ideal, an unreachable endpoint toward which we strive but at which we do not expect ever to arrive.[5] Thus, this interview study is not experimental social science, narrowly focused on a testable hypothesis that can be proved or disproved. Rather, it amounts to exploring a new landscape. It poses questions and seeks answers, using the sensibilities and best guesses of a dozen knowledgeable investigators, informed by the responses of the people interviewed.

This study is closer to ethnography than it is to experimental social science. Yet it diverges even from the majority of ethnographers, who have precise rules about how ethnographers are supposed to operate.[6] This study is closer to the "deep hanging out" that Clifford Geertz advocated in the latter part of his career than it is to the ethnography of anthropology textbooks.[7] All the investigators are insiders to Asian American communities. In some cases they were interviewing family and friends. In other instances, the respondents were new to them but nonetheless members of communities that recognized both interviewer and respondent as insiders.

With the exception of the initial author of this introduction (Paul Spickard), all the researchers and writers of this book are former students of Asian American studies at UC Santa Barbara. Some are now graduate students; others may be by the time this is published. It is customary for professors to use the minds and labor of students with minimal acknowledgment of those students' contributions.[8] By contrast, in the present volume the authors hope to offer credit where it is due. The colorism problem was first discussed in Asian American studies courses at UC Santa Barbara, particularly in Asian American Studies 137: Multiethnic Asian Americans. Yet all the participants had experienced this issue in their own Asian American families and communities of origin before they ever came to Santa Barbara.

So the method in this interview study is broadly exploratory, not rigorously scientific. It is not designed to achieve firm answers but rather to pose questions and suggest avenues for further inquiry. The general topography of the problem of colorism among Asian Americans is being charted. The small hills and valleys are not ready to be measured with any precision. That task—it is many tasks, really—is left to future investigators.

THEMES

The following are some themes that came up consistently in the interviews conducted.

Beauty Is Light

It was widely agreed that light-skinned people were more beautiful than dark people and that light skin was to be prized. A twenty-year-old Cambodian woman said:

> We grow up to look at Cambodians as people that are dark. . . . Traditionally beauty is basically when you're slender and light skinned. . . . My sister is dark-skinned and when we go to family functions, they always compliment me because I'm the lighter-skinned daughter and she doesn't get any [compliments]. . . . They always use the word *ime* to her, which means dark-skinned, but it's actually a negative word. Usually when they see light-skinned girls they say . . . *saroh* which means pure. . . . [or] *suhat* [meaning pretty].[9]

A fifty-eight-year-old Filipina woman reported that she and her darker sister were both raised by an aunt who preferred the light-skinned sister and said to the darker one:

You are so ugly, you are so black. . . . You are not like your sister who is prettier.

This she said to girls who were nine or ten at the time.[10]
A twenty-one-year-old Filipino man said,

I tend to look toward the lighter-skinned people, . . . because I prefer lighter-skinned girls. . . . When I was at the mall, there [were] three girls walking. I could tell the darker-skinned girl was the best looking out of all them, but my first glance or attention went toward the lighter-skin girl. . . . I've talked to a lot of Filipino girls out there and they all want to be light, because I think light is attractive and they think so as well.[11]

A nineteen-year-old Cambodian woman said she thought most of her American-born friends did not make skin color distinctions much,

But as for the older generation I think they have more of a preference. They think that the lighter-skinned Asian or Cambodian is prettier than the darker-skinned ones. . . . There's this one song in Cambodian . . . the man in the song sings out and he says that "You're dark and you're not that attractive because you're dark." Then the woman goes . . . "Yeah, I'm dark but I could be a good wife."[12]

Some people interviewed had other criteria for beauty besides light skin—hair color and style, eye shape (including enhancements—see chapter 5), body shape (including enhancements), a heart-shaped mouth. One nineteen-year-old Japanese woman declared that "Japanese and Koreans have tiny eyes" that need fixing.[13] A sixty-one-year-old Japanese man reported talking with his brother about a woman golfer:

Hiroshi mentioned that she would be beautiful but she has, you know—

and then he pulled sharply at the corners of his eyes.

Hiro said if she has surgery widening the eyes then she would be a pretty girl. . . . It's more easy to fall in love with. . . . lighter skin, round eye, is more pretty.[14]

A few Japanese and Koreans especially talked about skin texture. A thirty-one-year-old Japanese man said,

I don't know if it is so much color but more of a clear complexion. Not lighter more unblemished. Lighter would be preferred but not too dark.[15]

Some women mentioned they liked lighter skin because they felt it gave them more makeup options. Several interviewees told stories like this one, from a twenty-year-old Vietnamese woman:

My parents would pinch and rub the bridge of my nose to lengthen and thin it out when I was younger. . . . I have no idea where the nose thing comes from.[16]

Some men—well, a lot, actually—were uncouth. A twenty-two-year-old Taiwanese man said,

No [preference about skin color]. Just T and A.[17]

Even if there were other beauty considerations, almost everyone interviewed agreed that light skin was beautiful, a thing to be prized, and darkness was to be avoided.[18] Dark skin carried negative connotations. A twenty-one-year-old Chinese man said,

People probably prefer the lighter skin complexion as people might associate a dark skin as someone who is poor, dirty, or sluttish.[19]

A twenty-one-year-old Vietnamese man added this insight:

Dark Viet girls are more erotic, purely sexualized in the minds of men. Lighter skin indicates a more prestig[ious] woman.[20]

A nineteen-year-old Filipino said,

Darker people are wild[er] according to the general views of my ethnic and Asian group. Lighter people are more educated and sophisticated.[21]

Stay Out of the Sun

One prime method to attain lightness was to stay undercover. A twenty-three-year-old Chinese-Cambodian woman said:

I remember being younger and being told not to play outside too long because you'll look dark. Being dark is a bad thing.[22]

A thirty-three-year-old Chinese-Cambodian man reported:

I think because I'm dark. . . . During the summer, when I play sports outside . . . people would notice . . . and they react. . . . in a disappointing way. They say, "Aww, you're so dark." . . . You know that it's not a compliment. Even my girlfriend notices it. I have to remind her it hurts my feelings. . . . I would wear hats during the game or soon as the game was over, rest in the shade and not hang around outside and . . . I thought that if I put a mask on while I'm at home, like a ski mask, like a bank robber mask, that if you kept it on for the whole day . . . it would turn white.[23]

A twenty-year-old Cambodian woman said:

> My mom always tells my sister, "Come in, don't go outside because you're so dark" and . . . "aught sahot" [no more beauty]. . . . It hurts.[24]

A fifty-eight-year-old Filipina woman said:

> You will very seldom see Filipinos out in the sun. They are always under the shade. . . . Very few Filipinos go out swimming.

Why?

> Because you are out in the sun! You'll catch all these sun rays and you'll get black. No sunbathing![25]

A twenty-one-year-old Cambodian woman recounted:

> My dad said one day, "Don't wear shorts too much. You don't want to have dark legs, because no one will want to marry you." . . . Actually, with dark people, there tends to be a lot of jokes, like, "Oh, you might want to be careful or you'll turn into a *kaprik*, like a really black-black person." That's basically it or no one's going to want to marry you. . . . I get a lot of comments . . . from the older adults . . . like, "Careful, you're getting so dark. You better stay out of the sun."[26]

A thirty-year-old Filipina woman put it simply:

> Shun the sun! That's my sister's cry. Shun the sun! Shun the sun![27]

Don't Be Romantically Linked with or Married to Dark People

Many respondents reported their family members discouraging them from dating dark people. A twenty-three-year-old Chinese-Cambodian woman said:

> I used to go out with this dark guy and my dad said he was ugly. And that our kids would come out ugly.

She attributed this color prejudice to the Chinese community, of which she was a part, and said it did not exist in the Cambodian community, to which she was also connected.[28]

However, a twenty-one-year-old who reckoned herself purely Cambodian reported much the same thing:

> I remember this one time, I went to Kmart, and my mom saw this couple with children, and. . . . [she said], "Oh, look, he got himself a nice, white wife

and they have nice, white children." Like a light-skinned wife, that's what she meant. . . . She wasn't White, but she was Chinese, very light-skinned. . . . I have a Black boyfriend. So my parents do joke around a little bit, like if you guys have kids, your kids will be really dark and you have big puffy hair, and you're going to have funny-looking kids. But they don't really mean it that way. . . . they love him, though. They don't mean it offensively.[29]

A twenty-one-year-old South Asian woman reported being told,

Don't go out with dark-skinned people. My cousins . . . one was fair and the second was dark. The first one got married to a dark-skinned, skinny, rich man. The second married a light-skin, middle-class man. Since the first one was fair it didn't bother her that the man was dark, but the second one wanted a light person to compensate for her dark color.[30]

A fifty-eight-year-old Filipina woman, herself married to a White man, said:

You know, it's like they always say, *Improvar la raza* (Improve the race) [laughing], So . . . when you are looking for a mate, people are nice . . . but people can be rich also and be nice so why not go for the rich? So . . . why not go for the whiter? Why go for the darker, when your kids could be much better looking?[31]

Not Exactly Trying to Be White

There is overwhelming evidence that people who express a preference for light skin are not necessarily making a Whiteness move. That is, they appear not to be trying to look White, so much as they are hoping to look like upper-class people in their Asian country of origin. A twenty-year-old Chinese-Cambodian man told the interviewer:

I think if you're dark-skinned, that means you've come from ancestry that typically worked in the field and produced pigment, and so subconsciously they associate dark-skinned with labor and over time they associate attractiveness with upper-class people who happen to have light skin.

This man described himself as light-skinned and reported that his parents favored him over his darker brother.[32]

A thirty-three-year-old Cambodian-Chinese man said:

In the Cambodian community, the darker you are, it's associated with less intelligence, laziness, working manually and lower class, and unattractiveness. Business people are the lighter-skinned ones, more intelligent, more ethical, and morally superior. . . . I don't think they want to look White or Caucasian. I think they look down on Caucasian people so far as being morally inferior and White women have reputations as not being faithful. . . . They want to look [W]hiter because it's associated with wealth and status [in Cambodia].[33]

A twenty-two-year-old Cambodian-Chinese woman concurred:

Asians especially . . . Cambodians . . . associate dark skin with having to be a hard laborer, so you have to be in the sun and in the farm. . . . lower class and peasants . . . but if you're light-skinned that means you're well off and you can be in the house, and you don't have to work because your family's old money and . . . you have people to delegate it to. . . . I think my older relatives . . . associate lighter skin as being more pure, someone darker skin not being so pure, I guess kind of dirty. . . . I think it's because they want to look more upper-class than Caucasian.[34]

This is not just a Southeast Asian interpretation. A sixty-four-year-old Japanese woman called the desire for light skin a "Japanese aesthetic."[35] A fifty-one-year-old Japanese man asserted that "Lighter skin is associated with being ethnically Japanese."[36] A twenty-seven-year-old Japanese woman said that, if Japanese Americans wanted to be lighter, it was not that they wanted to be White:

No. Sometimes I think that about Japanese women because they bleach their hair and they have these whitening creams, but. . . . I think maybe it goes way back when . . . they used to have those Japanese theater, and they would paint their face white. It's not necessarily to look White. Maybe fair skin . . . looks beautiful to people. Not because they want to look White.[37]

Chinese, Koreans, Filipinos, and Vietnamese—women and men of all ages—reported that they saw the desire to have light skin as an old-country class move, not an attempt to be White.[38] Most would have agreed with this twenty-one-year-old Taiwanese man:

Light skin is the standard for beauty in Taiwan. . . . Wealthy people tend to be light-skinned, while darker people are associated more with low socioeconomic status. . . . I think people who prefer light skin want to be associated with [the] upper class, not because they want to be White.[39]

This is a complicated business, as suggested in chapter 1. This matter will be taken up further in chapter 4, where the layers of meaning and intention with regard to whether and to what extent the longing after lightness may or may not be a Whiteness move are sorted out.

Special Issues for Filipinos

Unlike other Asian nations, the Philippines had a 300-year history of European colonization under the Spanish, followed by a half century of formal U.S. colonialism, then another half century of U.S. neo-colonial domination. In common with other countries in Southeast Asia, the Philippines was host to a substantial Chinese minority. During the Spanish period, racial mixing was commonplace, albeit on terms of extreme social inequality between Spanish colonial masters and the indigenous population, whom the Spanish called *indios*. There were a substantial number of *mestizos*, though they were not formally assigned to a separate social class as were racially mixed people in South Africa or Brazil. Many of them had Chinese ancestry mixed in with the Spanish and the Filipino. Late in the Spanish period, European racial ideas of White biological and characterological superiority began to come to the Philippines and to shape race relations there in even more hierarchical ways.[40]

With such a history, it is reasonable to conclude that there may have been a racial longing after Whiteness—that is, after European features—included in Filipino preferences for light skin that would be different from the primarily class-derived motivation described previously for people from other nationality backgrounds. As Vicente Rafael has written, "mestizoness in the Philippines has implied, at least since the nineteenth century, a certain proximity to the sources of colonial power. . . . It is to cultivate a relationship of proximity to the outside sources of power without, however, being totally absorbed by them. . . . mestizoness comes to imply a perpetual and . . . privileged liminality: the occupation of the crossroads between Spain and the Philippines, Hollywood and Manila."[41]

Yet it might be premature to lay blame for this peculiarly Filipino development at the feet of social demographics of the Spanish era. The *ilustrados*, a late Spanish-era Filipino class of wealthy landowners, had many light members but also some dark ones. There surely was some racially derived color-class discrimination in the Spanish era. Eminent historian Teodoro Agoncillo wrote that "Between the *mestizo* and the 'native', there has been a barrier of feeling that borders on hostility. This feeling has its origin in the late Spanish period." But according to Agoncillo, the main color-ranking seems to have come later, during the era of American colonial hegemony, and the creation of a fairly large class he calls the "*mestizoisie*."[42]

U.S. colonial administrators, many of them military officers from the South, seem to have drawn American-style Jim Crow racial distinctions, including the taking of *mestizo* concubines by White soldiers in preference over darker women (the Americans included general Douglas MacArthur). So the racial marking of a biological sort that was begun in the Philippines late in the Spanish colonial era was intensified during the American period, in support of United States colonial domination.[43]

This colonial legacy—and its neo-colonial extension in postindependence movies, advertising, and television—may be reflected in the statements of some Filipinos about elements of European beauty standards lying behind the preference for light skin. A twenty-year-old Filipino reported:

> My mom. . . . has the internalization of the European beauty, high nose, light skin, etc. She grew up in the Philippines and the influence of Western culture (Spain and the United States) caused her to see Western beauty as the only true beauty. . . . Especially with the older adults, the lighter you are, the better off you are; the darker you are, the worse you are. They categorize people's social standing through skin color.[44]

A twenty-six-year-old Filipina said,

> My father suggested I have children with my White ex-boyfriend so he could have mestizo grandchildren. I think years of this colonial way of thinking and all the American propaganda has made it so that my father (and most other Filipinos) think that everything "'American'"—White American—is superior.

If she could choose her own skin color, she said, she would choose to be

> light, most definitely, so my family will shut up about how I look.[45]

Several of the Filipinos interviewed stressed their Spanish ancestry, and some would tell stories that had been passed down to them about it. This is not very different from the way an African American, like legendary scholar-activist W. E. B. Du Bois, proudly described his various European bloodlines (French, English, and Dutch) even as he proclaimed his Black identity.[46]

For all that there does seem to be something of a colonized Whiteness move behind some Filipinos' light skin preferences, it should be stressed that more Filipinos interviewed spoke of the working-in-the-sun class distinction than of a desire to be White or identified with Spanish or Americans. A few also pointed to regional physiological differences within the Philippines. A twenty-three-year-old Filipina characterized this as

> Filipino dark versus light Filipino . . . the Visayans in the south are discriminated against. They call us [Tagalog-speakers from Luzon] witches because we're light-skinned and we don't look like the other native Filipinos, like the Igorots that are really dark and barefoot . . . [47]

For other nationality groups, there was no evidence that the longing for lightness was a yearning to be White.

Special Issues around Chineseness

Color and ancestry issues are somewhat more complicated for people who identify themselves as Chinese and for those who have some Chinese ancestry. The Filipinos interv ewed frequently spoke of Spanish ancestry with pride, but they just as consistently omitted mention of their Chinese ancestry. This is quite different from others, such as Vietnamese, Cambodians, Burmese, and Thais. Like the Filipinos, many Americans from these countries have Chinese among their ancestors. Usually people from those other Southeast Asian countries would highlight, or at least admit, their Chinese ancestry.[48] Filipino Americans interviewed consistently chose to hide their Chinese ancestry. One thirty-year-old Filipina said:

> I'm very proud of my ancestry. The only thing I have a problem with is the Chinese part. I mean, I have Chinese blood and my family has Chinese blood and we have a Chinese family name; but we don't associate with the Chinese community because we are not accepted. Or at least I wasn't . . . because my skin was light, not in the yellow sense but in the [W]hite sense. . . . they had . . . slanty eyes. They looked Chinese whereas I don't look Chinese at all. . . . even though my last name was Chinese, I wasn't Chinese.[49]

Many Filipinos did not mention Chinese ancestry at all, even when they were questioned directly about it, and even when the interviewer knew from other sources that the person in question did in fact have some Chinese ancestry.

Some Cambodians with Chinese ancestry adopted a similar position of lack of solidarity with other Chinese people. They said it was because they perceived monoethnically defined Chinese people as racially prejudiced against them. A twenty-three-year-old Chinese-Cambodian woman told of her school years:

> Everyone there was Chinese and I sat in my group of four and there was this one Chinese girl . . . she went around asking everyone what nationalities we were . . . and I was like, "Oh, I'm Chinese and Cambodian" and she goes, "That explains why you're dark," but she didn't say it nicely. She said it like it was a slap in the face. . . . We don't want to be Chinese in this family, and even though we're more than half to 80 percent [Chinese], we've experienced a lot of racial discrimination by our pure Chinese relatives who look down on us for being part Cambodian and for being darker and poorer.

She noted that most Cambodians, in her experience, had some Chinese ancestry, but that nearly all emphasized their Cambodian identity and deemphasized any Chinese connection.[50]

Other people from Cambodia who had some Chinese ancestry lent support to this interpretation. Said one thirty-six-year-old Chinese-Cambodian woman:

I always think that Chinese is better than Cambodian.[51]

Many Vietnamese and Cambodian Americans have some Chinese ancestry, too, and showed the same range of engagement with that identity, from preferring to be seen as Chinese to referring to Chineseness as one piece of their complex identities and even denying the connection entirely.

Some Vietnamese Americans interviewed wrote a story of ethnic difference and primitiveness on Vietnamese people whose skin was in the darker range. They castigated darker-skinned Vietnamese as "Cambodians" and "jungle people." Most Cambodians had a sense of themselves as darker than Vietnamese, and so they did not reciprocate such sentiments in the same disdain-for-darkness terms, for all that they expressed ethnic dislike for Vietnamese people. It is perhaps worthwhile to point out that all these issues surrounding Chineseness were the legacy of ethnic issues and sometimes class issues within Asia and were not products of the encounter with the United States and European Americans.

A Link to Patriarchy

In the African American community, it has long been more important for women more than men to be light skinned, high nosed, and thin lipped. For men, financial, educational, or other status achievements could compensate for, even outweigh, a dark complexion.[52] One need look no further than the pages of *Ebony* to see that, in the magazine's regular celebrations of rich and beautiful people, the men presented as examples of success are, on average, quite a bit darker than the women.

In Black communities, as in most other communities, the primary enforcers of the beauty-status-eligibility code have been other women, frequently elder women of high status with a large stake in preserving the status quo.[53] One of the questions that the interviewers asked was, in Asian American communities, did people (particularly older women) tell girls more urgently than boys not to go out in the sun? Certainly, in *Mississippi Masala*, Harry Patel is as dark as Meena, but, as they say in Brazil, "money lightens," and so, perhaps, does maleness.

Our informants were unanimous that it was more important for women to be light than for men. A twenty-two-year-old Chinese-Cambodian woman put it well:

Definitely, I think that in the Cambodian community it's more important for the women and the girls to be lighter than the men. For the men it really doesn't matter what they look like, it's just a matter of what they do for a living and if they make a lot of money and if they come from a good family. . . . but I think for girls it's a lot of pressure to have that certain light skin look, like almost pale, deathly look. . . . definitely more pressure in almost any culture for the girls to look a certain way, to act a certain way, than for guys.[54]

Immigrants versus the American Born

The interview materials were quite consistent in supporting the suggestion that members of the immigrant generation and people in Asia have more (or at least more overt) colorism issues than do the American born. Some second-generation people claimed that they personally did not see any legitimacy to color issues (although some of those same people admitted they preferred to date lighter people), but they said that their parents in the United States or their relatives in Asia had strong colorism issues. A twenty-one-year-old American-born Cambodian woman said,

With the younger generation, they don't really have a preference. I mean, whatever they think is beautiful is beautiful, but as for the older [immigrant] generation I think they have more of a preference. They think that the lighter-skinned Asian or Cambodian is prettier.[55]

An eighteen-year-old Chinese woman said,

I think that once Asians become more assimilated, factors of one's skin tone become less significant. These mainstream [assimilated] Asians become more open minded and accepting of darker Asians since they are exposed to a more diverse group of people in America.[56]

A sixty-four-year-old Japanese woman agreed:

I think the Japanese American second generation mellowed their viewpoints. The first generation was more firm on light complexions.[57]

This pattern would lend credence to the interpretation that preference for light skin derives more from a desire to look like upper-class people in Asia than to look like White people.

A twenty-two-year-old American-born Chinese Cambodian woman recounted:

So when I was flying to Cambodia they had a Christian Dior booklet and they were selling the Snow White lightening creams, but when I was flying back to New York City they were selling tanning creams for Estée Lauder. . . . When I went to Cambodia . . . I was hanging out with my cousins . . . and they couldn't understand why I wanted to be tan because in America everyone wants a sun-kissed colored skin, and I couldn't understand why she wanted to be so white and light-skinned. But yeah everyone in Cambodia was covered up in hats and gloves and scarves even though it was 90 degrees, high humidity, sweating through everything . . . they literally had like face masks and stuff.[58]

A thirty-six-year-old Cambodian-Chinese immigrant woman agreed:

I don't think the Cambodians that are born here care about skin color. Most of them want [a] tan, they don't care about their skin color. Only the person that was born in Cambodia. They do care about their color.[59]

Color versus "Culture"

Frequently people interviewed slid back and forth between references to color and physicality on the one hand, and behavior and culture on the other. Sometimes this seems to have been an attempt at euphemism, to softly lay what is manifestly a racial judgment, not on the biologically essential, but instead on the more mutable behavioral. But often the interviewees actively associated other people's physicality with particular social or behavioral placements. For instance, a twenty-year-old Chinese-Cambodian man gave his relative the nickname "villager," because she was dark. When he thought someone's behavior was earthy, primitive, crude, or just excessively direct, he would say, "Damn, that's dark."[60] A twenty-year-old Chinese-Cambodian woman said, "If you're dark, it's like you know the language, and if you're lighter, people think you forgot the language."[61]

Interpreting Dark People as Immigrants

Frequently, our respondents laid a narrative of immigrant status on people whose skins were darker. As a twenty-year-old Chinese-Cambodian woman said, "The darker ones are like FOBs" (fresh off the boat).[62] This was consistently their interpretation of the status of Sarah, the dark-skinned young woman described in the second half of the survey.

Discrediting Light-Skinned People

Some people (especially from groups like Cambodians who are darker on average than most other Asians) look down on light-skinned people and presume they are ethnically less authentic and less loyal. A twenty-year-old Chinese-Cambodian woman complained:

> I'm lighter than them, and they think I'm selling out. . . . The girls don't want to talk to you because you're light but the boys want to get with you because you're light. . . . [The girls] think you're going to steal their boyfriends.[63]

This resentment seems to contain the connotation of wanton, predatory, or at least free sexuality on the part of light-skinned people.

One's Own Skin Color

In a classic study of colorism among African Americans, *Color and Human Nature*, W. Lloyd Warner, Buford H. Junker, and Walter A. Adams found that the people they interviewed consistently ranked their own skin color as lighter than the interviewers estimated it to be.[64] That pattern was not true among the Asian Americans interviewed for this study. The respondents seemed, rather, to calculate their own skin tones in relationship to other members of their families. For example, a twenty-year-old Chinese-Cambodian woman described herself as "light."[65] Her twenty-three-year-old sister, in a separate interview, agreed with that ranking, but described herself as "dark."[66] The interviewer estimated that, compared with other Chinese-Cambodians she had interviewed, the older sister was no darker than "medium," but she saw herself as dark because of the contrast to her sibling.

The people we interviewed were split: about half said that, if they could choose their own skin color, they would like to be lighter than they were;[67] about half said they would choose to be their same medium tone.[68] The older sister mentioned above said:

> I'd be light. I just think it looks better and cleaner.[69]

A few women said that they would like to be light or medium because that would give them more makeup options than if they were dark. Some went so far as to use skin bleaching agents to achieve their goal. A twenty-three-year-old Chinese-Cambodian woman said:

> I . . . go to the store and get a skin lightening to get more of an even tone. But I would like to be lighter. I think it looks better. You see the pretty girls on the karaoke videos and the magazines and they're all so much lighter.[70]

It may be worth noting that these particular media sources of beauty authority were generated in Asia, not in the United States. A thirty-six-year-old Chinese-Cambodian immigrant woman said:

I always want my skin to be white. I use some cream at night to bleach my face to make it light, but it never works out. . . . I used it almost a year and my skin is not that white.[71]

Skin lighteners are discussed in detail in chapter 4.

Choosing a Mate

Several people interviewed owned up to a frank desire to find a partner who was lighter than they were. A twenty-six-year-old Japanese man's expression was typical:

My personal preference I would tend to be on the lighter side. I wouldn't ever be with a dark-skinned person. . . . I guess that image of the princess with light skin.[72]

Some said they wanted someone White if possible. This was particularly true among Filipinos. A nineteen-year-old Filipino man said,

I've always wanted to be with White women, just the blond hair, the all-American look, blue eyes, tall.[73]

A fifty-eight-year-old Filipina immigrant who has a White husband expressed a clear plan to "improve the race" by marrying a White man.[74]

Only a couple of the people interviewed would have agreed with this twenty-one-year-old Chinese man:

Medium color looks the best to me. Too light makes me think I am dating a ghost. Dark tone is okay, but I prefer medium.[75]

But quite a few people expressed racial solidarity and a desire to marry another Asian, just one a little bit lighter than themselves. Said a twenty-two-year-old Chinese woman:

Medium, because I think that is the perfect color. . . . Light skin is okay, but too dark is out of the question.[76]

Children and Skin Color

The Filipina who wanted to "improve the race" tied her choice not only to racial status and personal choice but also to a desire for lighter children:

Why go for the darker, when your kids could be much better looking [lighter]? . . . I like fair skin guys. Well, because I have always been told I was

> dark so I guess in the back of my mind, have lighter kids so they won't suffer
> as much criticisms or . . . put downs as I received just because I was dark.[77]

A twenty-year-old Chinese-Cambodian woman prized her own lightness and
said that both she and her parents wanted a White or light-skinned boyfriend
for her:

> My mom—family—says marry a White guy so you can have tall, light
> kids. They say don't bring home a Black guy because he might steal your
> stuff. . . . They don't want me to marry a Cambodian guy. I'm guessing no
> Asians. . . . I would want a light husband. So my kids would be pretty. . . .
> Around here if you're dark, you're not really from higher class.

It is worth noting that this family did not hold out the hope for a light husband for their other, darker daughter. Presumably, she was so dark as to be
hopeless in their eyes.[78]

Even people who expressed Asian racial solidarity in their choice of
mates owned up to a desire for their children to be light. Usually they said
that they thought light children were better looking; sometimes they said
they thought that a light child would have an easier time making his or her
way in the world. The darkest anyone would go was this twenty-two-year-old
Chinese woman:

> Medium for my baby because light babies are okay, but dark is just ugly.[79]

A twenty-one-year-old Chinese-Vietnamese woman made the racial loyalty
connection explicit:

> My baby would be between light and medium, because it's close to White,
> which equals power, but not completely, which means roots.[80]

A twenty-year-old Cambodian-Chinese woman said that her family

> would rather have me have light-skinned babies. . . . I would love to have
> one child come out looking like they're mixed with Caucasian.[81]

A twenty-one-year-old Filipino was direct and prescriptive in his preference:

> If I were to choose . . . light babies are always attractive to me. . . . My kids, I
> don't want them to be dark. . . . Be like Michael Jackson, do something.[82]

What might someone do if their baby came out too dark? A twenty-
three-year-old Filipina described the extreme (see chapters 4 and 5 for some
other examples):

We have a Filipino friend and . . . her daughter came out dark, so what she did was she scrubbed her skin with scouring pads. Her daughter's skin, when she was a baby. She was dark-dark-dark-skinned, and she would scrub her skin all over her body with scouring pads, trying to, like—as if she was dirty. Like she was trying to clean off her skin. And now, the girl is twenty-something years old and she's got, like all over her skin it's as if she's got some sort of oil gland problem so her skin doesn't, her oil doesn't, you know, protect her skin any more because it's been rubbed off from damage so much. It's as if her entire body has a layer of callus on it from her mom doing this to her, abusing her. Just so she wouldn't be so dark. . . . and the dermatologists said, you, know, there's really nothing we can do. . . . she has no hair on her arms at all.[83]

A few people thought that a son could be medium tone, a bit darker than a daughter, "because light is more girlie."[84] Out of ninety-nine people interviewed, nobody hoped for a dark baby.

THREE WOMEN

A key part of each interview was to show the respondent pictures of three conventionally beautiful Asian American women: Jennifer, with light skin, hair, and eyes; Jane, medium in tone; and Sarah, quite dark.[85]

Figure 3.1. Jennifer

Figure 3.2.   Jane

Figure 3.3.   Sarah

The interviewer asked the respondent to make up a story about each of the women. Then young female respondents were asked to imagine that they could be any of the women and to tell which of the women they would most like to be. Young males were asked to tell which of the women they would most like to be romantically involved with. Members of the parental generation were asked, if they were to have a son, which woman would they most like their son to marry.

There are some limitations to this method. Ideally, we would have liked to present three pictures of men and to ask similar questions about them. But we initially had difficulty obtaining pictures of men that exhibited the range of phenotypes sought, and generally speaking the men we contacted were less interested than the women in the issues raised in the study. Moreover, the interviews were already quite long, each lasting well over an hour on average. To have added such a section based on men's pictures might have added insight to the study, but it would surely have made the interviews more difficult to conduct and analyze. We also note with regret that the questions in this section assume a normative heterosexuality and do not make an opening for questioning colorism in homosexual relationships. We regret these omissions and hope for future studies to flesh out the initial investigation we offer here.

Some people who have heard about this research have observed that the women are wearing different clothing and appear against different backdrops, and they have wondered if this might have biased the respondents' answers in some way. We think not. We have considered the matter at length and we cannot come up with a theory as to what direction the answers might have been biased by clothing, background, or facial expression. All three women wear clothing that is neutral, and they appear against neutral backdrops—a bush in two cases, a wall in the third. Few of the respondents made comments that seemed to be based on the women's clothing, and it was easy to filter out clothing-related responses when doing the analysis.

By the time the photograph stage of each interview was reached, the respondent knew that the issue under discussion was colorism. The interviewers might have taken pictures of the women in identical tee-shirts or with bare shoulders and blank expressions, but to have done so would have been artificial and would have lent a clinical air that we chose to eschew. To have taken such artificial steps seems a narrow pretense to science and might just as well have biased the respondents' answers in some other direction. Naturalness of clothing seemed to invite story. This exercise is more like the calling up of image and story by the Thematic Apperception Test than it is like experiments on lab animals.

It is not insignificant that, except for the senior investigator, all the members of the research and writing team are women. The issue of colorism first came up in the courses Paul Spickard taught on interracial romance and marriage and multiracial people at UC Santa Barbara. About two-thirds of the students in those courses, as in other Asian American studies courses at UC Santa Barbara, usually are women. Spickard attempted to get some men students involved in this project, but none were interested. What is more, when colorism issues were posed in class exercises, male students tended to give shallow answers that did not explore issues with much interest or sophistication. It may be that the fact that beauty is a concern laid more on women than on men makes sensitivity to colorism issues more a woman's issue than a man's issue. Or it may be that Asian American men are more inhibited than Asian American women about self-expression. Or again, it may be that Asian American men feel they have more substantial matters on their minds. Whatever the case, the gender cast to this research is inescapable.

Jane, the Medium-Toned Woman

Some respondents marked Jane with a particular ethnicity, usually Chinese or Korean. All saw her as wholesome, hip, the All-Asian-American Girl. No one took her for an immigrant; all insisted she was American born. A twenty-year-old Chinese-Cambodian man said:

> She looks smart, she comes from a middle-class family, and she looks like she can be popular, happy. . . . I could see this girl pulling up to a library in a 2002 Honda Civic.

—a new model of the stereotypical Asian American status car.[86] A twenty-one-year-old Filipino had an only slightly different take:

> I think she goes to a pretty good school, Cal State or whatever. She looks like a UCI [University of California Irvine—an Asian majority school] type of chick or a [University of Southern California] type of chick and I think she's living off pretty okay. I can see her driving a Beemer. I can see her going to bars and stuff, just chilling with her friends. I can see her at the mall shopping for clothes.[87]

A twenty-two-year-old Chinese-Cambodian woman said:

> She comes from a good family. She seems very happy, very confident, very self-contained . . . very easy-going.[88]

A twenty-three-year-old Filipina said

> She seems more sophisticated, and she's got her life more together.[89]

A twenty-two-year-old Vietnamese man said she

> looks like an educated girl. . . . probably a rich girl.[90]

A twenty-three-year-old Chinese-Cambodian woman said:

> She's outgoing and friendly and she has a warm vibe. She seems like she comes from a happy family. . . . she looks like somebody with a good head on her shoulders.[91]

A thirty-year-old Filipina had a very specific vision of Jane:

> Fashion conscious, she looks like the typical . . . South Coast Plaza Asian. . . . all black, tailored stuff, the more expensive the brand name the better.[92]

Jennifer, the Lighter Woman

Several respondents noted the possibility that this woman might be racially mixed, but most did not remark on that possibility. Most of them believed her to be younger than the other two, although all three young women were in fact within a few months of each other in age.[93] Only one thought she was an immigrant.[94] And most of the respondents saw the light-skinned woman as shallow and troubled.[95]

A thirty-three-year-old Chinese-Cambodian man had quite a lot to say about the light woman and her character:

> kind of on the superficial side. . . . Average student, just drifting through school, not really as ambitious. . . . She likes to go clubbing and she feels like if she's not with somebody, then there's something missing in her life so she kind of goes from guy to guy trying to find that right guy but sometimes guys that are nice to her she doesn't really appreciate that much, because she's superficial so she's looking for flashy guys.[96]

A fifty-two-year-old Filipina said:

> This woman is trying too hard because she colored her hair. She. . . . wants to shed her Oriental roots by becoming blond.[97]

A twenty-two-year-old Chinese-Cambodian woman said:

> She . . . didn't rigorously challenge herself. . . . I feel like she had a lot of opportunities. . . . [she] goes surfing and hangs out with her friends and listens to music and goes to concerts. She seems very laid back.[98]

A twenty-year-old Vietnamese woman said,

> She doesn't have that image of the super-intelligent Asian kid.[99]

A twenty-three-year-old Cambodian-Chinese woman wrote a story of dysfunction on Jennifer's features:

> she doesn't seem as smart. . . . not as rich. She seems poorer to me and she seems like she has more problems, more internal problems. . . . she seems younger and almost like lost. . . . she's had a hard life. . . . it just seems like she's having issues about herself. . . . I can see her having behavioral problems in class . . . and I can see her being rebellious at home.[100]

A thirty-year-old Filipina said:

> She's someone who's trying to fit in. . . . torn between one culture to the next.[101]

A twenty-three-year-old Chinese-Cambodian woman said:

> She probably gets hurt a lot from guys who are just curious.[102]

A sixty-year-old Filipino said,

> She has had a very unhappy life.[103]

The attribution of a troubled nature to light-skinned Jennifer may be an outgrowth of that hoary myth in American race relations: the theme of the tortured multiracial person, torn between two races and cultures, and dysfunctional because of the conflict. The consensus of both scholars and community observers is that such an attribution is hogwash, but still the myth persists.[104]

Sarah, the Darker Woman

The people interviewed had by far the most to say about Sarah, and they told a detailed, remarkably consistent story. Some of the respondents marked her ethnically as Filipina or Cambodian. Almost everyone marked her as older than the other two women. Almost universally they saw her as an immigrant, as the oldest child in her family, as quiet, conservative, responsible, and virtuous. A twenty-year-old Chinese-Cambodian man said:

> I see her . . . [as] someone who's coming from a family who hasn't been in America long. . . . she looks like she works hard.[105]

A thirty-year old Filipina said:

> She seems shy, very appearance conscious. . . . She is first generation im-
> migrant . . . fresh off the boat . . . she just got here. . . . very obedient, very
> rooted in family. . . . someone who still values the traditions.[106]

A twenty-year-old Chinese-Cambodian woman said:

> she's supposed to be ghetto, but she pulled herself out. . . . I think she has
> strict parents. . . . She has to take care of her brothers and sisters.[107]

A twenty-year-old Filipina said that Sarah

> just came from the Philippines and she probably has a boyfriend back there
> in the Philippines, in the boonies somewhere. She's smart. . . . And her fam-
> ily is strict, and they have rules. . . . I think she has a job to support herself
> and . . . to make herself and her family more comfortable in America.[108]

A twenty-three-year-old Chinese-Cambodian woman said:

> She looks really innocent. . . . She looks like she would be the oldest child
> in the family. She's a really nice girl so she's responsible for a lot of things,
> like the big sister type. . . . Disciplined and respectful.[109]

An eighteen-year-old Chinese woman said:

> She looks less Americanized. She also looks kind and in comparison to
> the other [lighter] girl, she has this innocence about her. . . . She probably
> comes from a not as wealthy background as the other girls and I think
> that she's really close to her family. She looks like she probably could be
> an immigrant. . . . She looks like she'd be intelligent, but I probably don't
> think that her English is as fluent as the other girls'. I think that she is
> bilingual and that she probably speaks her language at home because of a
> very strong cultural identity and I picture her coming from a pretty large
> family. . . . I could see her being the caretaker of the family. . . . the center
> of family life.[110]

A thirty-three-year-old Cambodian-Chinese man offered a detailed picture
of Sarah:

> She's a very good student, maybe around a 3.7 GPA, 3.8, but she doesn't
> think that much outside the box. . . . working really hard to support her
> family. She has a couple of younger brothers and sisters, and she's the only
> one that's working and so her parents are poor so she has to support the
> family and go to school, and she's doing all that very well because she ac-

cepts hard work as part of her life. . . . 1.5 or first generation. . . . She seems
the most genuine."[111]

Several people used the term "FOB" or "fobby"—as in "fresh off the
boat"—to describe the dark woman. A twenty-three-year-old Chinese-Cambodian woman said:

> She looks like she's a nice girl, like she knows English even though it's not
> that great. And she looks like she's very studious and almost constrained,
> but like the typical FOB.[112]

A twenty-two-year-old Chinese-Cambodian said:

> She's very strong but seems very nice at the same time, has very good
> manners, seems very polite but is a very strong woman. Perhaps she was a
> first generation immigrant. She saw hardship through her family but saw
> her family overcome it so she has a resilience factor and she's a very hard-
> working, determined individual.[113]

A twenty-year-old Cambodian-Chinese woman put the story all together:

> [Sarah] is very much Cambodian. She has that darker skin tone, her hair
> looks a little bit thicker. She looks very sweet. She looks very innocent. She's
> even more so in touch with her background. . . . like if she were twenty,
> she'd have the innocence of being fourteen years. . . . She goes to school
> with the Cambodian mentality. She also comes home with the Cambodian
> mentality that a girl is supposed to be put in her place in the kitchen, clean-
> ing and watching the kids. . . . She lives in a small house in the middle of,
> closer to downtown Long Beach [a dense concentration of Cambodian
> Americans]. . . . She doesn't strike me as being rich at all, or even middle
> class. . . . I could see her dropping her bag after class or after whatever,
> automatically going to the kitchen to help mom or grandma, making food,
> cooking for her dad or her brothers and setting up things ready at the din-
> ner table. . . . She's just watching kids, or brothers and sisters.[114]

It should be unnecessary to add that, although the respondents wrote
quite consistent stories onto the features of these three young women, there is
no particular relationship between those stories and the three women's actual
lives—in fact, they are quite different.

Whom Would You Choose?

The interviewers asked young women: If they could to choose to be any of the
three women in the pictures, which woman would be their first choice, which

second, and which third—and why? Thirty-eight young women responded. They ranked Jane, the medium-toned woman, first, with an average ranking of 1.4. Jennifer and Sarah were tied at 2.3, quite far behind. By far the most women put Jane as their first choice. Jennifer, the light woman, seemed audacious, uncontrolled, perhaps even dangerous. Dark-skinned Sarah seemed staid, boring, and conservative. They wanted to be somewhere in between.

A half-dozen ranked Sarah first; those people all ranked light Jennifer last. Most of these were Asian American studies majors. In Asian American studies, there is a lot of negative discussion about Asian women seeking after White men, and there is some sympathy expressed for the plight of dark women. There seems to have been a racial loyalty element for some of the Asian American studies students who chose Sarah first. The converse was also true: a half dozen chose Jennifer first; those people ranked dark Sarah last. Most of these women were not from the Asian American studies crowd and were not party to the discourse of ethnic solidarity to the same degree. They seem to have been embracing the lightness without the critical layer of race loyalty that was present for the Asian American studies majors.

When the interviewers asked young men (twenty responded) whom they would most like to date or marry, the answer was somewhat different. Once again Jane, the medium-toned woman, was the clear leader, at 1.4. Sarah came in second, at 1.9. She was the clear second choice of older men in their late twenties and perhaps early thirties, who were weighing the question with more seriousness, as if choosing a life partner. Several remarked that dark Sarah reminded them of their mothers. Jennifer, the light woman, came in last at 2.2. Younger men, in their late teens and early twenties, and non-Asian American studies students tended to choose Jennifer second after Jane. Often they did so with a leer and a wink, suggesting that they thought she was a loose woman with whom they would like to spend a hot weekend. But Jane was someone they saw as a more serious candidate for life partner.

The preferences were even more marked among the twelve members of the parental generation who responded to this question. Jane was again the first choice, with a 1.3 ranking. But the distance between the other two increased. Sarah was the solid second choice, at 1.8, for a reason that a fifty-two-year-old Filipina made clear: "That's the one that will keep values, family values."[115] As the quotes in the previous section indicate, dark Sarah was viewed as traditional, subservient, and filial—an ideal daughter-in-law. By contrast, no one wanted light Jennifer, whom they saw as troubled. She rated a 2.9, and all but one parent ranked her dead last.

There seems to be a contradiction here. The people we interviewed expressed a clear, consistent preference for light skin in the abstract—for themselves, for their potential life partners, and for their children. But when asked which of the three women they would prefer to be, to date, or to have for a daughter-in-law, they did not choose the light woman, Jennifer. They went for medium-toned Jane instead. For all that they expressed an abstract yearning after lightness, when confronted with the actual possibility, nearly everyone turned away from it and toward an intermediate position. And parents, at least, clearly did not quite trust someone who was light. They preferred the dark.

One aspect of these findings to pause and consider is how the perceptions about female Asian Americans changed the assumptions that respondents attached to darker skin. Typically, dark-skinned people are seen as unintelligent, savage, and uncivilized. Some of these assumptions stem from the idea that these people are not natural parts of the local landscape. For example, many of these respondents assumed that Sarah, the darker-skinned woman, was an immigrant. However, they did not mark her as savage. Although many assumed that English was her second language, they saw her as hard-working and possessing high moral values. On one hand, her dark skin marked her as a foreigner. On the other, her status as an Asian female civilized her and exempted her from being seen as savage. It is the interviewers' guess that the assumptions would have been different if the dark woman had been identified as Black or Latina.

NOTES

1. Paul Spickard wrote this chapter. Research was conducted by Monica Chum, Holly Hoegi, Lynn Kawabe, Helen Lee, Akshata Mankikar, Paul Spickard, and Charmaine Tuason.

2. May Yu Danico, *The 1.5 Generation: Becoming Korean American in Hawai`i* (Honolulu: University of Hawai`i Press, 2004).

3. James V. Spickard, "Slow Journalism? Ethnography as a Means of Understanding Religious Social Activism," PRPES Working Papers #36, Program in Religion, Political Economy and Society, Weatherhead Center for International Affairs, Harvard University, September 2003.

4. Clifford Geertz, "Thick Description: Towards an Interpretive Theory of Culture," in *The Interpretation of Cultures* (New York: Basic, 1973), 3–30.

5. James V. Spickard, "On the Epistemology of Post-Colonial Ethnography," in *Personal Knowledge and Beyond: Reshaping the Ethnography of Religion*, ed. James V. Spickard, J. Shawn Landres, and Meredith B. McGuire (New York University Press, 2002), 236–52.

6. James P. Spradley, *The Ethnographic Interview* (Belmont, CA: Wadsworth, 1997); Robert M. Emerson, Rachel I. Fretz, Linda L. Shaw, *Writing Ethnographic Fieldnotes* (Chicago: University of Chicago Press, 1995); Robert S. Weiss, *Learning from Strangers: The Art and Method of Qualitative Interview Studies* (New York: Free Press, 1995); Irving Seidman, *Interviewing as Qualitative Research*, 2nd ed. (New York: Teachers College Press, 1998); Margaret D. Lecompte and Jean J. Schensul, *Designing and Conducting Ethnographic Research* (Walnut Creek, CA: AltaMira,

1999); Stephen L. Schensul, Jean J. Schensul, and Margaret D. Lecompte, *Essential Ethnographic Methods: Observations, Interviews, and Questionnaires* (Walnut Creek, CA: AltaMira Press, 1999); David M. Fetterman, *Ethnography Step by Step*, 2nd ed. (Thousand Oaks, CA: Sage, 1998).

7. Clifford Geertz, "Deep Hanging Out," *New York Review of Books* (October 22, 1998): 69–72.

8. See, for example, Sucheng Chan, ed., *Hmong Means Free: Life in Laos and America* (Philadelphia: Temple University Press, 1994).

9. Appendix 2, Interview (hereafter Int.) number (hereafter no.) 9. Transcripts of all the interviews are in the files of the colorism project, in the office of Prof. Paul Spickard, Dept. of History, University of California, Santa Barbara.

10. Int. no. 25.

11. Int. no. 28.

12. Int. no. 31.

13. Int. no. 43.

14. Int. no. 52.

15. Int. no. 55.

16. Int. no. 64.

17. Int. no. 66.

18. E.g., Int. nos. 11, 30, 32, 36, 45, 53, 57, 58, 59, 62, 63, 71, 73, 74, 78, 84, 85, 86, and 87.

19. Int. no. 37.

20. Int. no. 70.

21. Int. no. 80. Some people, of course, found this alleged wildness attractive. A twenty-two-year-old Filipino-Chinese man reported, "My friends like dark-skinned Filipinos, because they say they are far more exotic and sexier than light-skinned Asians. Most of the girls at import car shows are dark-skinned, voluptuous Filipinas"; Int. no. 62.

22. Int. no. 5.

23. Int. no. 6.

24. Int. no. 9.

25. Int. no. 25.

26. Int. no. 30.

27. Int. no. 27. Also Int. nos. 28, 31, 32, 35, 36, 64, 78, 80, 87, and 89.

28. Int. no. 5.

29. Int. no. 30.

30. Int. no. 87.

31. Int. no. 25. Also Int. nos. 28, 57, 62, 63, and 78.

32. Int. no. 1.

33. Int. no. 6.

34. Int. no. 7.

35. Int. no. 39.

36. Int. no. 51.

37. Int. no. 50.

38. Int. nos. 10, 26, 29, 30, 31, 32, 35, 43, 53, 56, 58, 59, 60, 64, 80, 85, 86, 89, and 95.

39. Int. no. 37.

40. Edgar Wickberg, "The Chinese Mestizo in Philippine History" *Journal of Southeast Asian History* 5 (1964): 62–100; Teodoro A. Agoncillo, *History of the Filipino People*, 8th ed. (Quezon City: Garotech, 1990), 121–22 and *passim*; Barbara M. Posadas, *The Filipino Americans* (Westport, CT: Greenwood, 1999), 5–7; Renato Constantino, "The Miseducaton of the Filipino," in *Vestiges of War: The Philippine-American War and the Aftermath of an Imperial Dream, 1899–1999*, ed. Angel Velasco Shaw and Luis H. Francia (New York University Press, 2002), 177–92. On South Africa and Brazil, see George M. Fredrickson, *White Supremacy: A Comparative Study in American and South African History* (New York: Oxford, 1981); Anthony W. Marx, *Making Race and Nation: A Comparison of the United States, South Africa, and Brazil* (Cambridge, U.K.: Cambridge University Press, 1998).

41. Vicente Rafael, *White Love and Other Events in Filipino History* (Durham, N.C.: Duke University Press, 2000), 165–67.

42. Agoncillo, *History of the Filipino People*, 4–5.

43. Stanley Karnow, *In Our Image: America's Empire in the Philippines* (New York: Ballantine, 1989), 267–70; Catherine Ceniza Choy, "Asian American History: Reflections on Imperialism, Immigration, and 'The Body'" in *Pinay Power: Peminist Critical Theory*, ed. Melinda L. de Jesús (New York: Routledge, 2005), 81–97; Rene G. Ontal, "Fagan and Other Ghosts: African-Americans and the Philippine-American War," in *Vestiges of War*, ed. Shaw and Francia, 118–33.

44. Int. no. 82.

45. Int. no. 78. Also Int. nos. 92, 94, 96, and 97.

46. W. E. B. Du Bois, *Dusk of Dawn: An Essay toward an Autobiography of a Race Concept* (1940; repr., New Brunswick, N.J.: Transaction, 1984), 11–20, 97–117.

47. Int. no. 89. A twenty-one-year-old Chinese man insisted that Han Chinese were lighter and therefore of higher status than native Taiwanese or Mongols; Int. no. 53.

48. See, for example, Joseph Cheah, "Negotiating Race and Religion in American Buddhism: Burmese Buddhism in California," (PhD diss., Graduate Theological Union, 2004); Jiemin Bao, *Marital Acts: Gender, Sexuality, and Identity among the Chinese Thai Diaspora* (Honolulu: University of Hawai`i Press, 2005).

49. Int. no. 27.

50. Int. no. 8.

51. Int. no. 10. Also Int. nos. 30, 62, and 84.

52. Kathleen Russell, Midge Wilson, and Ronald Hall, *The Color Complex: The Politics of Skin Color Among African Americans* (New York: Harcourt Brace Jovanovich, 1992); Obiagele Lake, *Blue Veins and Kinky Hair: Naming and Color Consciousness in African America* (Westport, CT: Praeger, 2003).

53. Naomi Wolf, *The Beauty Myth* (New York: Harper Perennial, 2002); Patricia Buckley Ebrey, *The Inner Quarters: Marriage and the Lives of Chinese Women in the Sung Period* (Berkeley: University of California Press, 1993); Lois Banner, *American Beauty* (Chicago: University of Chicago Press, 1983); Take Sugiyama Lebra, *Japanese Women: Promise and Fulfillment* (Honolulu: University of Hawai'i Press, 1984).

54. Int. no. 7. Also Int. nos. 9, 26, 28, 30, 31, 34, 43, 53, 58, 85, 86, and others.

55. Int. no. 31.

56. Int. no. 32.

57. Int. no. 39.

58. Int. no. 7. More on the marketing of skin lighteners in chapter 4.

59. Int. no. 10. Also Int. nos. 3, 6, 36, 40, 43, 45, 53, 56, and 59. Independent corroboration comes from Deborah Johnson, a social worker and activist in international adoptions. She reports a color selectivity factor at work in which children are kept and which put up for adoption outside of the country. She has traveled to many countries, including Korea, China, India, the Philippines, and Peru, visited adoption agencies, and helped adoptees and their American families learn about the cultures from which the young people were adopted. She says that, in every country she has visited, the light-skinned babies are almost all adopted locally. The dark-skinned babies are left for the international adoption market. Deborah Johnson, conversation with Paul Spickard, July 26, 2005.

60. Int. no. 3.

61. Int. no. 4.

62. Int. no. 4.

63. Int. no. 4.

64. W. Lloyd Warner, Buford H. Junker, and Walter A. Adams, *Color and Human Nature* (New York: Harper and Row, 1941).

65. Int. no. 4.

66. Int. no. 5.

67. E.g., Int. nos. 31, 32, 35, and 36.

68. E.g., Int. nos. 34, 59, and 70.

69. Int. no. 5.

70. Int. no. 5.

71. Int. no. 10.

72. Int. no. 41. Also Int. nos. 29, 34, 53, 62, 70, and 80.

73. Int. no. 95.

74. Int. no. 25. Also Int. nos. 32 and 36.

75. Int. no. 37.

76. Int. no. 57. Also Int. no. 59.

77. Int. no. 25.

78. Int. no. 4.

79. Int. no. 57. Also Int. no. 62.

80. Int. no. 70.

81. Int. no. 36. Also Int. nos. 31, 32, and 34.

82. Int. no. 28.

83. Int. no. 89.

84. Int. nos. 40 and 80.

85. These names are pseudonyms.

86. Int. no. 1.

87. Int. no. 28.

88. Int. no. 7.

89. Int. no. 89.

90. Int. no. 83.
91. Int. no. 8.
92. Int. no. 9. Also Int. nos. 29, 30, 32, 35, 36, 57, 62, and 74.
93. E.g., Int. nos. 42, 55, 89, and 94.
94. Int. no. 36.
95. Int. nos. 29, 32, 36, 62, 64, 80, 83, and 96.
96. Int. no. 6.
97. Int. no. 24.
98. Int. no. 7.
99. Int. no. 75.
100. Int. no. 8.
101. Int. no. 27.
102. Int. no. 5.
103. Int. no. 97.
104. For assertions of the tortured racially mixed image, see Edward Byron Reuter, *The Mulatto in the United States* (1918; repr., New York: Negro Universities Press, 1969); Reuter, *Race Mixture* (1931; repr., New York: Negro Universities Press, 1969); Everett V. Stonequist, *The Marginal Man: A Study in Personality and Culture Conflict* (New York: Russell and Russell, 1937); Jon Michael Spencer, *The New Colored People: The Mixed-Race Movement in America* (New York: New York University Press, 1997). For correctives to such silliness, see Paul Spickard, *Mixed Blood: Intermarriage and Ethnic Identity in Twentieth-Century America* (Madison: University of Wisconsin Press, 1989); Maria P. P. Root, ed., *Racially Mixed People in America* (Newbury Park, CA: Sage, 1992); Root, ed., *The Multiracial Experience* (Thousand Oaks, CA: Sage, 1996); G. Reginald Daniel, *More Than Black? Multiracial Identity and the New Racial Order* (Philadelphia: Temple University Press, 2002); Teresa Williams-León and Cynthia L. Nakashima, eds., *The Sum of Our Parts: Mixed Heritage Asian Americans* (Philadelphia: Temple University Press, 2001); Kip Fulbeck, *Paper Bullets* (Seattle: University of Washington Press, 2001); Naomi Zack, ed., *American Mixed Race* (Lanham, MD: Rowman and Littlefield, 1995); Pearl Fuyo Gaskins, *What Are You? Voices of Mixed-Race Young People* (New York: Henry Holt, 1999); Lise Funderburg, *Black, White, Other: Biracial Americans Talk About Race and Identity* (New York: Morrow, 1994); Marie Hara and Nora Okja Keller, *Intersecting Circles: The Voices of Hapa Women in Poetry and Prose* (Honolulu, HI: Bamboo Ridge Press, 1999); Kevin R. Johnson, *How Did You Get to Be Mexican? A White/Brown Man's Search for Identity* (Philadelphia: Temple University Press, 1999); Loretta I. Winters and Herman L. DeBose, eds., *New Faces in a Changing America: Multiracial Identity in the 21st Century* (Thousand Oaks, CA: Sage, 2003).
105. Int. no. 3.
106. Int. no. 27.
107. Int. no. 4.
108. Int. no. 35.
109. Int. no. 5.
110. Int. no. 32.
111. Int. no. 6.

112. Int. no. 8.

113. Int. no. 7.

114. Int. no. 36. Also Int. nos. 28, 29, 30, 31, 53, 57, 62, 74, 80, 83, 84, 89, 94, 95, 96, and 99.

115. Int. no. 24.

· 4 ·

Making a Better Me?
Pure. White. Flawless.[1]

$\mathcal{T}$wo women stop by a cosmetics counter at a major department store in downtown San Francisco to shop for skincare. One woman looks like she had recently suffered severe burns over most of her face. The middle part of her face looks normal, but the rest of her face has large, burned areas that look like they are going to peel off—almost like a scab that is ready to fall off. The burns look excruciatingly painful. She seems to be okay, but one cannot help but wonder what happened to her. Was she in a major accident? Was she in severe pain? How long has she had this condition? In a casual conversation with her girlfriend, the woman explains that the burns on her face were the result of a chemical peel.

An advertisement in *Preview*, a popular beauty magazine in the Philippines, features a Filipino woman's face. She has jet-black hair, haunting almond-shaped ebony eyes, full rose-colored lips, and glowing white skin. The advertisement is for a product called "SkinWhite" and it reads, "Get 99 percent whiter, better."

In July 2003, an article in the *Philippine Daily Inquirer* reported that over two million units of skin lightening soap are sold annually in the Philippines.[2] Less than a year later, a survey about skin lightening usage conducted by Synovate, a research firm, revealed that among its respondents in the Asia-Pacific region, the Philippines reported the highest rate of usage with 50 percent of the respondents stating that they currently use skin-lightening products.[3]

Although the examples cited illustrate the overwhelming popularity of skin lightening products in the United States and Asia, little research has been done to examine the relationship between the marketing and usage of skin lighteners across the Pacific. Simply put, skin lightening is a process in which one uses a cream, scrub, or other substance that will inhibit the body's ability to produce melanin or lighten the body's natural skin color. Skin

79

lightening is not a natural process, as it requires using products that interfere with the body's natural function, one of which is to produce melanin. Also, skin lighteners on the market have been known to contain potentially fatal ingredients, such as mercury. It is a process that is important to take notice of, because the use of cosmetic skin lightening products has risen tremendously in recent years. Such products can be found everywhere from the local grocery store to high-end cosmetics counters and the offices of most dermatologists. Although both men and women use such products, as with most cosmetics products, they are far more often used by women, so marketing is targeted mainly at women.

This chapter will begin by taking a brief historical look at what prompts people to use skin-lightening products and how these ideas affect Asians and Asian Americans. How such products are marketed by comparing two sets of advertisements is then examined. The interest is in exploring how ideas of light skin change or are maintained across national borders. How communications media contribute to the spread of ideas favoring light-skinned images and the use of skin lightening products will also be examined. Finally, the chapter will end with a brief discussion of the risks involved when using skin lighteners.

CHANGING THE COLOR OF YOUR SKIN

During the formation of the American republic, the assembly of all White founding fathers had to decide what the connection of race and nationality would be.[4] The architects of the American republic envisioned a place for *The Lovely White*—where the truest and highest morals and standards were to be upheld.[5] The idea of the Lovely White became the new foundation for beauty and morality. However, how could there be a republic of the Lovely White when Blacks and Native Americans were in the picture?

Benjamin Rush, an intellectual and leader in American medicine, believed that Blacks should be included in the new republic. He believed that dark skin was a disease, and that, like any other disease, it could be cured. For Rush, the correct cure would help incorporate Blacks into the new republic, and medicine provided the means to a cure. The prescriptions that Rush used to whiten Black people's dark skin were similar to the treatments he recommended to clients who were suffering from what he called "diseases of the mind." He believed that, "due to the wonderful magic of medicine, a harmonious future awaited all mankind." By curing Black people's skin disease, "The entire society would be whitened: the people of the new nation would be more 'homogenous.'"[6]

Although notions of Whites as superior and non-Whites as inferior and savage existed long before the American Revolution, the idea of civilizing non-Whites created a profound power dynamic in the United States and abroad. However, it must be noted that ideas about race are a series of intricate meanings that are constantly changing through political struggle.[7] Therefore, race has more to do with power than it does about actual human difference. Michael Omi and Howard Winant assert that "there is no biological basis for distinguishing among human groups along the lines of race. . . . race is a matter of both social structure and cultural representation."[8] Although there is no biological or scientific basis to race, the idea of race is still used as a political tool to assert the power of one group over the other.

Over time, the myth of Whites as superior has turned Whiteness into an investment that has a particular cash value. Like any other investment, the high value of Whiteness is maintained at the expense of the subordination of non-Whites.[9] This is an important point, particularly for Asians in the United States and abroad, because this relates to perceptions of light-skinned versus dark-skinned Asians, where skin color itself has a social and political value (as mentioned in chapter 3).

In short, the idea of the Lovely White has evolved to mean more than what Rush believed to be a biological flaw or what determined one's beauty and morality. Instead of curing a disease of the mind to incorporate non-Whites into the American landscape, Whiteness has become a commodity in which one can now invest. Notions of the Lovely White (or the lovely light) have taken on various meanings, particularly when the images and beauty expectations of Asian women in the United States and abroad in a capitalist-driven, technologically savvy world are considered.

THE SEDUCTIVE POWER OF SKIN LIGHTENING

It is difficult for one to walk around in everyday life and not be influenced by the images encountered—from the ultra-beautiful people on the television and movie screens, the billboard advertisements along city streets, and the plethora of websites one encounters, the messages are intoxicating:

> "In just five minutes, the power to restructure your skin."
> "For a pure, white, flawless complexion."
> "To be really beautiful, don't forget to whiten."
> "Results in weeks? Try seconds."
> "Now lighten your skin from within."

"Have you ever wondered how come so many Black, Asian and Indian celebrities are all very light skinned? . . . Research for 'Skin Whitening' was undertaken with the aim of creating a product that would help dark-skinned individuals to attain a lighter and fairer complexion tone. . . ."[10]

In her book *Beauty Secrets: Women and the Politics of Appearance*, Wendy Chapkis explains: "Indeed, female beauty is becoming an increasingly standardized quality throughout the world. A standard so strikingly White, Western, and wealthy it is tempting to conclude there must be a conscious conspiracy afoot."[11]

Contrary to popular belief, skin lightening is an age-old practice. Women in the United States were using skin-lightening lotions (homemade and manufactured) as far back as just after the Civil War.[12] Ironically, these products were used primarily by White women who felt that maintaining a certain look helped reflect their social status. Having light skin implied that one was a woman of high class, education, and leisure. A woman's light skin meant she did not need to work outdoors to make a living. "A light complexion preoccupied not only the educated in science and letters, but it was also the governing aesthetic across the social spectrum."[13] To White women, these products were to help enhance or refine their features, which helped them maintain their racial and class superiority. The products also allowed White women to construct their own sense of control over their definitions of beauty and femininity. Many of these products were touted to help enhance their skin by brightening it or removing freckles and dark spots from the face.

For Black women, advertisements for skin lighteners were in the Black press by the 1850s.[14] However, the ways in which these products were marketed to White and Black women differed greatly. Many of the skin lightening advertisements for Black women featured the progression of a dark woman becoming lighter, promoting the idea that these products could help these women drastically change their overall appearance.[15] By doing so, they could change (not maintain) their social status. Peiss explains:

Women might purchase a skin whitener that covered and colored the skin and simultaneously disclaim its status as paint. For women of European descent, whitening could be absorbed within acceptable skin care routines and assimilated into the ruling beauty ideal, the natural face of white genteel womanhood. . . . For African Americans, the fiction was impossible: Whitening cosmetics, touted as cures for 'disabling' African features, reinforced a racialized aesthetic through a makeover that appeared anything but unnatural.[16]

What made skin lightening different for Black women was that the beauty standard that was imposed on them was based on Eurocentric standards and did not help them climb the social ladder. Rather, it enhanced their subordination by forcing Black women to strive for an impossible ideal—a racial transformation—while allowing White women to retain their power. Another thing that made skin lightening alluring for Black women was that lighter-skinned Black women tended to be part of the middle class. Instead of trying to erase their Blackness, many used skin lighteners in hopes of showing their status as middle-class Black women.

Like Black women, Asian women fall into a similar trap. For many Asians the implicit message that they are fed each day of their lives is simply that they are not White enough. Their noses are not pointed enough, eyes not big enough, and although pale, their skin is not the right kind of light. Granted, there are brief moments when it is okay to be Asian—like when Jackie Chan's latest film is number one in the box office, Michelle Yeoh is cast in the newest James Bond film, Lea Salonga is given high praise for portraying a Vietnamese prostitute in Broadway's newest hit, or when America's least likely American idol, William Hung, signs an album contract before his fellow idol competitors do. Even then, these brief moments have more to do with Whites upholding their power and honoring their own internalized perceptions of who Asians are and should be, as opposed to the idea that Asians should actually be proud of who they are via their own definitions.[17] In the meantime (and just to be safe), Asians should aim to be better, lighter, and Whiter than they already are. Besides, even when Asians are granted the spotlight, the likelihood of these Asians looking like you or me is slim. It is okay to be Asian in the media as long as you are the right kind of Asian: small in stature, pale skinned, and large eyed; with a perfect eyelid and a refined nose; and of course, no look is complete without blonde highlights.

These controlling images are quite compelling. Patricia Hill Collins states that "controlling images are designed to make racism, sexism, poverty and other forms of social injustice appear to be natural, normal, and inevitable parts of life."[18] While images of lighter-skinned successful people (including lighter-skinned Asians) continue to grace the covers of magazines and messages, such as "Now lighten your skin from within" travel through the Internet and make the desire to lighten seem normal, it should be remembered that these messages are instruments of power used, not necessarily to help Asians improve their state of being, but for corporations to profit. For example, ten years ago, it was uncommon to see skin-lightening products at the local department store cosmetics counter. Today, every major cosmetics company has some form of skin lightener. In the end, the rise in popularity of skin lighteners has less to do with one's actual need for it and more to do with profit a company can have by creating a demand and actually supplying the product to consumers.

In his discussion of the covert nature of Whiteness, Lipsitz asserts that people are surrounded by notions of Whiteness in their everyday lives. However, it is difficult to pinpoint because we are so inundated by it to the point that Whiteness is normalized. [19] For example, women believe that what they see in the media is beautiful because they see the same type of images often enough that they seem natural. Susan Bordo, in *Unbearable Weight: Feminism, Western Culture and the Body*, echoes a similar sentiment when she asserts that representations of women in the media homogenize and normalize notions of beauty to the point that altering oneself to uphold such standards also goes without question.[20] This is especially significant today, as magazines such as *New Beauty*, Vicki Belo's *Skin*, and others like them become new staples on newsstands all over the world, and as China announces its first "Miss Plastic Surgery" contest [21] Finally, when was the last time one went channel surfing without running into a show where someone is going under the knife or touting the latest laser-chemical-all-natural skin remover? These images seep into the minds of women everywhere, telling them that altering oneself is natural. It's as if natural beauty does not exist at all, because beauty these days can only come prepackaged and even mechanized. Unfortunately, the power of the images is so strong that it seems there are no questions about the political or health implications of using products, such as skin lighteners, because the industry and consumers alike take desired Whiteness for granted. Zdena, a woman who grew up in the Czech Republic, elaborates, "if you can get people to buy the image, they spend most of their day trying to get the goods, not thinking about the politics."[22]

Although Asians do not constitute a large sector of the popular media, the beauty pressure for Asian women to lighten their skin is high. Through independent and ethnic-specific media, there is a growing number of Asian American–specific beauty magazines, such as Los Angeles–based *Audrey*. There are large Asian-based cosmetics companies, such as Shiseido and Shu Uemura, which cater specifically to an Asian and Asian American clientele. Additionally, smaller, direct sales companies, such as Esolis (which is now defunct), DHC, Pola, and Noevir, tout their products and send their catalogs to Asian and Asian American prospective consumers.[23] Because they are smaller companies and focus on direct sales, they are not typically found in major stores. Each of the cosmetics companies mentioned above has a line of skin lightening products. Shiseido's line is called *UV White*. Shu Uemura has a line called *Whitening Essence*. Esolis had the *Sol White Brightening System*. DHC has a specific line for skin brightening. Pola features the *Whitissimo* line. Noevir has a product called *Pure Whiteness*. These brands claim to target the specific needs of Asian skin. For example, Esolis's primary target market was Asian American women. An introductory letter from the Esolis president Tari E. Reinink explains:

Let's face it, there are clear differences between Asian and Caucasian skin, and it's likely you have been frustrated at finding the right skin care products that work for you. . . . Esolis products address the specific needs of Asian skin including dark spots, uneven skin tone, oiliness, breakouts and skin sensitivities. Our products use clinically proven technologies to illuminate and brighten your skin, repair and protect it from the sun, restore moisture and reverse the signs of aging.[24]

In terms of who actually uses products, there seems to be a divide between immigrant consumers versus non-immigrant consumers. Non-immigrant Asian women tend to veer away from the skin lightening products, whereas immigrant women tend to opt for them, even looking to use the same skin lightening products they were accustomed to using in their native country (it is common to see skin lightening products in Asian grocery and beauty stores). The issue of the immigrant versus American-born color complex will be addressed briefly. Asian Americans (whether they would like to recognize it or not) have a particular privilege within the Asian and Asian American color hierarchy. Working behind the cosmetics counter, this author has observed that Asians who seek out skin lighteners (like the customers mentioned at the beginning of this chapter) tend to be part of the immigrant generation. Because they are caught in the middle—between Asia and the U.S.—there is a tendency to be influenced by the beauty standards from their native country, which, as has been seen in the advertisements, valorize light skin. These ideas travel to the United States when these women immigrate.

The desire for light skin among these women is a double-edged sword because, on one hand, light skin is seen as beautiful in their native country. At the same time, when they come to the United States, the image of a typical American is usually of one who is White. This adds another layer of pressure for immigrant women to be light-skinned. Peiss incorporates a similar discussion in her book when she states that daughters of immigrant parents tend to use cosmetics to look more American. This is because it helps them (in their own eyes) to assimilate and become part of the landscape of the newly adopted country.[25] This analysis is carried further by considering the power of U.S. colonization in a country, such as the Philippines, and how status symbols change depending on locale. Immigrant generations have a particular idea of what success should look like. In their native country (in this case, the Philippines), success is defined by light skin because it illustrates that one is not part of the laboring class and does not have to work under the hot sun to make a living. [26] The look of success in the United States is a different story, because, as an industrialized nation, most people already work indoors. Tan skin in the United States is a marker of the leisure class because it implies one was vacationing.[27]

One's status as an American in effect lightens one's status regardless of skin color, at least in the eyes of many Asian immigrant women. Although many Asian Americans tend to be perplexed by their fellow community members wanting light skin, they do not recognize that their own desire to keep or even darken their skin is a part of the same colonial process. Hence, many Asian Americans who shun skin lightening may opt for the opposite beauty product and invest in tanning. Because tanning involves skin darkening, many believe that the process symbolizes going back to a natural state of being. Tanning may give Asian Americans a sense of ethnic authenticity and can possibly allow them to believe it is natural for them to be tan (even if they obtained the tan through artificial means). A second-generation Filipino student said, "I don't understand why my mother tries so hard to be light. She uses tons of skin bleaching products from the Asian grocery store, while I'm here trying to get a decent tan."

A critical look at this complex reveals that tanning and lightening are two sides of the same coin. Beauty is part of one's class identity, but it must be remembered that the markers of class identity change depending on where a person is. In the end, it is the beauty industry that profits from the idea that one's class has a particular look and that look can be invested in their products.[28] This complex is one that leaves immigrant Asians disadvantaged and longing for a particular class status (which many immediately equate to skin color) and elevates Asian Americans, because they have a particular class status regardless of their skin color. Asians in the United States and abroad are all part of this color complex.

SELLING LIGHTER SKIN:
THE ADVERTISEMENTS IN ASIA AND THE UNITED STATES

In countries such as the Philippines and Thailand, it is not uncommon to see major advertisements for skin lightening products with such blatant slogans as:

> "Get 99 percent whiter, better."
> "For a perfectly fair, even, and radiant complexion within four weeks."
> "Flawless, timeless skin. Get armed and radiant."
> "The expert whitening mask for bright skin, like glowing from within."
> "The safest, fastest, and most natural method available for whitening overall skin color and fading age spots, liver spots, freckles, hyperpigmentations, and skin discolorations."
> "Now . . . a cleanser that can help lighten brown spots or discoloration, as it deep cleans. Can also help brighten any complexion."[29]

Usually, these advertisements will feature Asian women with glowing white skin, jet-black hair, and delicate almond-shaped obsidian eyes. The messages in these ads are clear, as they tend to be more racially blatant in content: It's okay to be Asian, but you must be light, have big eyes, and a body that is at least twenty pounds lighter than average. It seems that these are the requirements for entertainers in Asia and to some extent, people who sell such products (they are, after all, representing these cosmetic lines).[30] Like the advertising in the United States, Asian cosmetics advertisements promise that people are simply one product (or a series of products) away from perfection.

During a recent trip to Thailand, researcher Lilynda Agvateesiri made this observation:

> As I walked through the malls, I observed the many faces behind the counters. After several weeks of stay and numerous strolls though department stores, I observed what I had suspected: Most of the sales people in the upscale department stores had lighter skin than the sales people elsewhere. This was especially true for the women in the cosmetics departments where I spent most of my time doing research on skin lightening products. This came as no surprise to me. Cosmetics companies want to employ people who can represent the look that the companies are trying to sell, and in Thailand, they are trying to sell whiteness.[31]

Agvateesiri is correct. These companies are trying to sell whiteness, but a particular kind of whiteness. Although many may think that Asian women use skin lighteners to become White or European, this is not necessarily true. As a skincare consultant and someone who has worked in the cosmetics industry for a number of years now, this author has spoken to many women who use such products. In listening to them explain why they seek out such products, many of them are indeed satisfied with being Asian or having Asian features. In fact, they like being Asian because it gives them a distinct and unique identity. However, they just wish their features were a little bit "better." While they would not trade in their dark, silky hair or almond eyes for blonde hair and blue eyes, they are looking to clean up or refine their look. In short, they are looking to become better versions of themselves. While these women want to retain their Asian-ness, their ideas of a better Asian are related to Whiteness, because it seems that they are looking to be Asian as seen in the White imagination (again, with ultra-white skin, a double eyelid, jet black straight hair, and such). In other words, they are looking to be Asian according to White standards of beauty.

Looking back, ideas such as the ones that Benjamin Rush promoted during the formation of the American republic still translate to contemporary society—especially with relation to race, power, and Whiteness. What does this mean for Asians and Asian Americans? Mia Tuan, Eduardo Bonilla-

Silva, and others have pointed out that Asian Americans have achieved in the minds of many White Americans a position they call "honorary Whites." Stereotyped as high achievers who value family and education, they are sometimes called a "model minority"—people who act like Whites and who are not threatening to White hegemony. [32] Although the status of Asian Americans as honorary Whites is usually explained in terms of culture, one must question if this may also have something to do with skin color. Are Asian Americans considered the model minority in part because their skin color is closer to Whites than to Blacks? If Asian and Asian American skin, like Black skin, is a disease, is using a cosmetic skin lightener a way to cure this disease?

The answers to these questions are long, complicated, and go beyond U.S. borders. The connections between Asians and Asian Americans and skin lightening are carried into the international sphere when the correlation between skin lightening abroad and skin lightening in the United States and how marketing is targeted specifically to Asian and Asian American women is examined. To help look at these connections, a series of skincare advertisements will be compared. The first set is from two L'Oreal products from the Philippines: a sunscreen called *UV Perfect* and an exfoliating mask called *White Perfect*. The second set of images is from a catalog by a now defunct company called Esolis. Based in the United States, this company's target audience was Asian American women. The sections of the Esolis catalog called "For women who are serious about brightening their skin" and "Targeted solutions, intensive treatments" will be examined. Both sections focus on the *Sol-White Brightening System*.

The Philippine advertisement for L'Oreal's *UV Perfect* (see Figure 4.1) was featured in two popular magazines: *Preview* and *Cosmopolitan* (Philippine edition). It is a two-page spread featuring a Portuguese-Chinese movie star from Hong Kong, Michele Reis. The left side of the advertisement features her covering a part of her face, as if she were blocking something. The right side of the advertisement shows a photo of the actual product (the product is about a quarter of the size of Reis's face on the opposite page) and the text reads as follows:

> Technological breakthrough in UV Protection: For the first time in a daily care regimen, the ultra powerful association of Mexoryl SX + XL against harmful UVA and UVB to prevent skin darkening. Activa cell to stimulate skin's natural repairing process. Maximum pleasure: Ultra-light and quickly absorbent UV Perfect creates an unnoticeable screen on your skin leaving it soft, smooth and matte. Dermo-Expertise. From research to beauty. Because you're worth it.

This ad focuses on the actress's face and less on the product. Reis's look is racially ambiguous. To advertisers, she is White (with some exotic features).

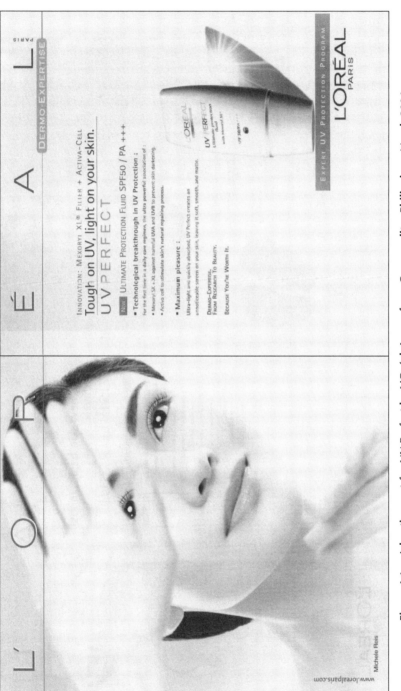

Figure 4.1. Advertisement for UV Perfect by L'Oréal. Image from *Cosmopolitan* Philippines, March 2004.

To audiences in the Philippines, she is Asian (with some European features). This allows the L'Oreal advertisers to believe that they are embracing a new kind of beauty; one that is not Eurocentric and allows women in the Philippines to relate to her Asian face and at the same time aspire to her measure of Whiteness. Her face or her beauty represents a type of *relatable ideal*. With that, advertisers can claim that Reis's beauty is universal and speaks to many women on various levels because she is racially ambiguous. Additionally, they can claim that she represents not difference but sameness. However, in a commentary about Saira Mohan, a Punjabi-Irish-French model who was deemed the "new global beauty" by *Newsweek* magazine, Margaret Hunter states:

> The paradox of purporting 'global' beauty to a woman who could be mistaken as 'European, European, or European' seems an obvious contradiction. But this is the paradoxical discourse of the new beauty regime. It is simultaneously inclusive, multicultural, and new, while remaining exclusive, Eurocentric and old. The 'new global beauty' as Mohan is called in the article is in fact old-fashioned, white beauty [re]packaged with dark hair. This means that beauty, and thus capital, is still elusive for many women of color as it continues to be defined by primarily Anglo bodies and faces.[33]

Hunter's point is reflected in this advertisement and L'Oreal's deliberate positioning of Reis as their representative for this product. Reis has ultra-white, glowing skin, which contrasts with her black hair and dark almond-shaped eyes. She is beautiful enough to be marketable yet exotic enough for the everyday woman in the Philippines to identify with her.

While advertisers probably chose Reis because she is a relatable ideal, this image instead creates difference, especially for women who read the advertisement. Judith Williamson, in her article "Woman Is an Island: Femininity and Colonization," explains: "Our culture, deeply rooted in imperialism, needs to destroy genuine difference, to capture what is beyond its reach; at the same time, it needs constructs of difference in order to signify itself at all."[34] Reis's face does exactly this for the L'Oreal ad; because she is an Asian, it is assumed that women in the Philippines (or women who read these particular magazines) can relate to her features. Reis symbolizes the ideal that women should strive for by investing in these beauty products. In the end, consumers will never become like Reis. When they invest in these products, consumers are in turn investing in the idea of what they fantasize they might become and not in the actual result of the products. In a recent survey of the popularity of skin lightening products, 41 percent of respondents who reportedly used such products stated that they had noticed little or no difference in their skin as a result.[35] Despite this reality, consumers continue to invest in the idea of achieving lighter skin.

When all is said and done, Reis does not represent sameness. Rather, she symbolizes a skin color hierarchy that has existed for hundreds of years. In her discussion of the beauty queue, Hunter explains:

> The beauty queue explains how sexism and racism interact to create a queue of women from the lightest to the darkest, where the lightest get the most resources and the darkest get the least. The lightest women get access to more resources because not only are they lighter-skinned and therefore racially privileged, but their light skin is interpreted in our culture as more beautiful and therefore they also are privileged as "beautiful women." The conflation of beauty and light skin is part of how racial aesthetics operate —lighter-skinned people with more Anglicized features are viewed by most in American culture (either consciously or unconsciously) as superior.[36]

While advertisers try to position Reis as a relatable ideal, they instead reveal a power dynamic that is prevalent in the Philippines: Light skin is indeed a marker of higher class, but that light skin is not necessarily limited to European or American definitions. Light skin because one is partly Chinese (or other East Asian) is also a marker of higher class. Hunter's notion of the beauty queue, translated to the Philippines, is not limited to just a Black-White spectrum. It also includes East Asians as lighter skinned and more racially privileged than darker-skinned Filipinos. This dynamic can also explain why many public figures, such as entertainers and politicians, in the Philippines tend to be light-skinned and look like they have part-East Asian or part-European ancestry.[37]

In comparison, the Esolis catalog section, "For women who are serious about brightening their skin," also features a racially ambiguous model (see Figure 4.2). Though she could pass for Asian, she has slightly darker skin than other models in the catalog. Also, the other models have features that are more distinctly Asian. Unlike the *UV Perfect* ad, the Esolis catalog focuses more on the product and makes it so that the product and text are the relatable elements, and the model's face presents the problem as opposed to the solution. The model is slightly darker-skinned and is looking up—she represents the consumers who, as the caption states, are "serious about brightening their skin." It seems that her racial ambiguity marks her inauthenticity. Hence, if she brightens her skin, she could possibly be "more" Asian than she already is.

This catalog excerpt focuses on the product and the text, which emphasizes the uniqueness of Asian skin and the need for products that specialize in such areas. Like the *UV Perfect* ad, the problem posed in this catalog is hyperpigmentation.

Unique Brighteners Specifically for Asian Skin

Hyperpigmentation and related problems like freckles, dark spots, and uneven skin tone are caused by exposure to the sun. The sun triggers a chemical reaction within your skin that produces the enzyme tryosinase, which in turn stimulates the production of melanin, the substance that causes your skin to darken. Esolis scientists have addressed this natural biological process by developing products that brighten your skin's appearance.

Most brightening products available today are either too weak to be effective or not gentle enough for delicate Asian skin. Esolis offers you the

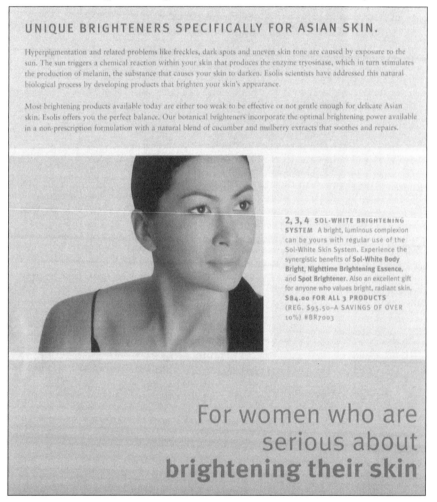

Figure 4.2. "For women who are serious about brightening their skin." A catalog excerpt featuring the Sol-White Brightening System by Esolis. Image from April 2003 Esolis product catalog.

perfect balance. Our botanical brighteners incorporate the optimal brightening power available in a non-prescription formulation with a natural blend of cucumber and mulberry extracts that soothes and repairs.[38]

When all is said and done, both advertisements position darkness as a problem, even though the Esolis catalog recognizes hyperpigmentation as a natural biological process. Whether these products use botanical or scientifically developed ingredients, both see whitening or brightening as the solution to preventing darkness. Hyperpigmentation is simply a pseudoscientific euphemism for the skin getting darker, particularly through sun exposure. Therefore, these advertisements read a lot like early skin bleaching advertisements that were marketed to Black women in the mid-1850s in which the product was seen to enhance White features. "In the case of white women, their skin-bleaching practice is represented as a limited and medically necessary practice designed to remove 'dirty marks' and 'blemishes' from the white female bodies. Dirty marks, blemishes and freckles which, if not removed, could put in question the racial purity of the white supremacist race."[39] If we examine some of the main terms used in the text of *UV Perfect* and Esolis marketing—flawless, radiance, purify, brightness, clarity, perfection, luminous, even, softer—they imply the Lovely White beauty standard, but they are imposed this time on Asian and Asian American women.

The product in the Philippine advertisement is sunscreen. In the United States, when a sunscreen is advertised, the product is usually positioned as something that protects the skin. For example, an advertisement for a sunscreen called *UV Plus* by Clarins claims that it leaves the skin "strongly protected against UVA and UVB infrared rays, skin's youthful appearance is preserved." An equivalent sunscreen in the Philippines is marketed in a different way, because instead of focusing on protection from harmful sun rays, it centers on the ideas of correcting and repairing bad—that is, dark—skin. The *UV Perfect* ad focuses on skin darkening as a problem that needs to be fixed. Hidden behind this text is the notion of saving these consumers from their fate of being dark and savage-like. Aging is not their problem; skin cancer is not their problem; their skin color is their problem. In typical colonial fashion, it takes science to right the wrong of their skin color. By using mostly pseudo-scientific jargon, such as the new and innovative ingredients Mexoryl XL Filter + Activa Cell, the product is used to prevent skin darkening and stimulate skin's natural repairing process. The highly advanced, scientific ingredients are used to lighten the dark-skinned consumers, and Reis poses as an example of that possibility. Ultimately, women in the United States use the Clarins sunscreen to be protected. Women in the Philippines use the L'Oreal sunscreen to be perfected as defined by old colonial standards.

The Esolis catalog focuses more on the product and the text, which emphasizes the uniqueness of Asian skin and the need for products that specialize in such areas. Like the *UV Perfect* ad, the problem posed in the catalog is also that skin gets darker. The text is quite deceptive because it softens its pseudo-scientific jargon to emphasize the unique and delicate nature of Asian skin. This is different from the *UV Perfect* ad, which is heavy with pseudo-scientific jargon. It seems that the Esolis catalog positions science as an inadequate means to address the delicate nature of Asian skin, because to treat Asian skin, one must employ methods that are naturally and spiritually sound. Although this may seem reasonable to some, what this really does is reiterate stereotypical Orientalist thinking, which sees Asian women as delicate lotus blossoms and situates Asian culture as meditative, at one with the earth, and imbued with mystical ancient medicinal practices. With that, both advertisements position darkness as a problem (even though the Esolis catalog recognizes that hyperpigmentation is a natural biological process), and both see whitening or brightening products as the solution to preventing darkness. Whether these products use botanical or scientifically developed ingredients, using them is a justifiable solution to a process that occurs naturally in the body.

The next product looked at is featured in a two-page L'Oreal advertisement from the Philippines for a "deep whitening mask" called *White Perfect* (see Figure 4.3). The ad reads:

> Innovation: Triple Melanin Block Concentrate. The expert whitening mask for bright skin, like glowing from within. White Perfect. A cream mask for a complete action on skin fairness, radiance and transparency. (1) Intense whitening mask: triple concentrated Melanin Block helps regulate melanin production. (2) Facial Massage: Microbeads help exfoliate dark dead cells from skin's surface to boost skin brightness. Instant proven results: More radiant + transparent skin. 97% of women agreed. Smoother, more even skin tone. 93% of women agreed.

In this ad, the racial connotations are quite blatant: (a) Darkening can and must be stopped (through the triple melanin block concentrate). (b) Lightness is more than just skin deep. In fact, it must come from within. Lightening is not limited to the skin; it must come from other facets of one's being. (c) Lightening can happen instantly and is something that many women aspire to and can achieve. These are all assumptions that go unquestioned.

That a major worldwide company, such as L'Oreal, can sell an expert whitening mask clearly illustrates that race does matter. Race is used to create a problem that many cannot change: their skin tone. At the same time, the quest to erase one's racialized features has become a profitable commodity. This study is not implying that everyone has fallen into the trap of desir-

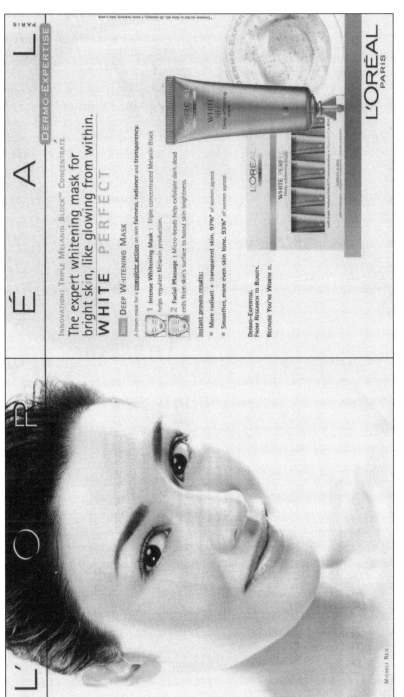

Figure 4.3. Advertisement for White Perfect by L'Oréal. Image from *Cosmopolitan* Philippines, March 2004.

ing light skin. However, it is important to note that, for some, the social, economic, and political benefits of light skin are too difficult to pass up. This is reflected in an editorial featured in the *Philippine Daily Inquirer* titled, "Whiteners Won't Transform 'Morena' into 'Mestiza.'"[40] Writer Lora Gahol begins, "No amount of whitening cream will turn caramel tint into milk." What starts as a realistic and progressive view on skin lighteners takes an unexpected turn when she attempts to make the distinction between bleaching and lightening.

> Bleaching is designed to make the skin lighter than its original color, thus the need for strong chemicals. Whitening, on the other hand, only tries to bring back the skin tone you had as a baby. . . . Morenas and true-blue Pinays, though they may have to give up dreams of alabaster skin, reap considerable benefits from whitening preparations. The products help to improve dramatically skin texture and generate glow. Whitening is for everybody. And the great news is everybody can find a product to suit her budget and skin type. Local manufacturers and affiliates of high-end international labels have released their own versions of the highly popular skin-care preparation, giving consumers more and more choices.[41]

Similar to the messages the *White Perfect* ad sends out, Gahol's commentary illustrates how light skin has become a marker of success and a worthwhile investment. Her commentary uses some of the same tropes the advertising uses, such as the notion of light skin signifying a journey back to one's natural state. Promoting the idea that lightness is natural is how some companies and consumers can justify using a skin lightener. As Gahol explains, whitening is natural, for the process entails bringing back the skin tone you had as a baby. On the other hand, bleaching is unnatural, because it alters one's original skin tone. Hence, that process should be shunned! One must pose the question: Is there really a difference between whitening and bleaching? Absolutely not. If one were to compare the ingredients in whitening and bleaching products, one would find the same types of ingredients.

On the surface, the racial connotations in the Esolis catalog are not as blatant as the *White Perfect* ad. However, in the "Targeted solutions, intensive treatments" section, the model featured has the darkest skin among all the Esolis models (see figure 4.4). Her head is bowed as if in shame. The implication is that she should be ashamed of being so dark. She needs special help—intensive treatments—because she is especially unattractive and not allowed to show her full face until she has sought this help. Like the previous Esolis excerpt, the model represents the possible consumer. If so, what does this say about darker-skinned Asian American women? And why the urgent need for intensive treatments? Also, in the larger scheme of things, although comparatively darker-skinned to the others in the catalog, the model fea-

Figure 4.4. "Targeted solutions, intensive treatments." Another catalog excerpt featuring the Sol-White Brightening System by Esolis. Image from April 2003 Esolis product catalog.

tured is really not that dark compared to the spectrum of Asian skin tones. The implication is that most Asian American women are in desperate need of help.[42]

Catherine Lutz and Jane Collins, in an exploration of the popular magazine *National Geographic*, explain how racist assumptions have become a part of popular belief: "Like other forms of essentialist reasoning, racist thought has the appeal of simplicity, and it draws authority from invoking biology and nature."[43] It is unfortunate that this seems to be the popular sentiment regarding skin lightening, especially in the Philippines, other parts of Asia, and among Asian Americans of the immigrant generation. As mentioned previously, skin lightening is a multimillion dollar industry in the Philippines and other areas of Asia. However, it needs to be recognized that these ideas are not natural. Rather, they are related to a longer colonial history. The false notion that Filipinos should desire white skin was created by several hundred years of Spanish and American colonial history. This idea is so ingrained that it becomes accepted as if it were a cultural norm. Many cosmetics companies have taken advantage of these ideas and have turned them into an entire industry. For example, David Gosling, president and managing director of Avon India Beauty Products, states that "Fairness creams are trendy throughout the Asia-Pacific. People here basically want lighter skin. Culturally, fair skin is associated with positive values that relate to class, lifestyle and beauty."[44] Light skin is made possible without critically examining the racist implications behind it. The single colonial narrative of light skin being better becomes the colonial truth. The ability to Whiten knows no color.

Gahol's previous commentary also celebrates the accessibility of light skin: that everyone regardless of their income level can reap the benefits of going back to a natural state of lightness. Deborah Root notes that, "Consumption is power, and the ability to consume excessively and willfully becomes the most desirable aspect of power."[45] Along similar lines, Williamson states that capitalism creates the idea that everything (including one's social position) can be bought and exchanged.[46] The power of consumption is something that must be considered because possessing light skin alone does not symbolize power. That one can buy light skin and even be excessive about the buying is another symbol of power. This is mentioned because it cannot be assumed that only dark-skinned people use skin lighteners—especially when these products are advertised so widely—to the point where light skin becomes a common desire for *everybody*. Peiss explains:

> Beauty may have been considered the birthright of only wealthy or fortunate women in the nineteenth century, but cosmetics advertising sold the idea that an attractive appearance was an accomplishment all could easily achieve. Mail-order and tabloid-style ads promised cheap, instant beauty to working women unable to afford the time and money leisured women spent on beauty culture.[47]

Therefore, even if one was not born into money, one could appear to be of a higher social standing by simply looking the part. While this may not actually change one's social standing, it allows the working class to feel as if they have escaped their social station, even if only temporarily.

Finally, the type of language used to promote skin lightening does not limit its market to only dark-skinned consumers. This can be seen in the *White Perfect* ad's usage of main phrases, such as bright skin, radiance, and smoother, more even skin tone. In her discussion of the double meaning of particular words in beauty advertisements, Peiss explains that the use of a word such as *bright* implies changing the skin's condition by smoothing out its texture, as well as turning dark skin into a lighter shade of brown.[48] The meanings differ according to where particular advertisements are featured. The Philippine ads use whitening as a main marketing phrase; the U.S. ads replace it with brightening. That way, U.S. advertising can incorporate the same racially charged messages but in a more covert way. According to the advertisements, Asian women in the United States do not whiten their skin (to do so would be to insinuate that they were participating in some type of ethnic cleansing ritual). Instead, they brighten to improve radiance, prevent aging and hyperpigmentation (these are the same main phrases that are found in most skincare literature in Asia). Peiss explains, "This use of the word bright had a double meaning: By smoothing rough or uneven skin, creams did brighten, in a sense, by improving the reflectivity of light, but among African Americans the term had a distinct connotation, that of light brown skin."[49] Again, while the idea of having radiant and luminous skin is appealing, one must ask, what are the racial implications behind such terms? In truth, to brighten and to whiten are different sides of the same coin. Advertisers have just learned to adapt the jargon to the population they are trying to target.

DANGEROUS BEAUTY

As alluring as lightening one's skin may seem, there are numerous harmful side effects to using skin lighteners, including cancer and even death. This is quite scary because these products can be acquired anywhere—from the local drug store to a high-end department store to a doctor's office. Early skin lighteners were dangerous. At first, many were homemade concoctions and people did not know how safe or effective these products or ingredients would be.

> American Negro women of the nineteenth century sometimes rubbed lye directly on their skin, and others applied harsh acidic products made for removing dirt and grime from floors and walls. There were also homemade concoctions of lemon juice, bleach, or urine to smear on the skin and arsenic wafers to swallow, all designed to "get the dark out."[50]

Early manufactured products used highly poisonous ingredients, such as lead and mercury. In extreme cases, women died because of overuse of these products. [51] When mercury enters the body, it can affect the bones, nervous tissue, and blood. "Along with sight or hearing loss and hand tremors, high doses of mercury can trigger personality changes, anxiety, irritability, insomnia, general fatigue, memory loss progressing to cerebral palsy, and potentially fatal kidney failure."[52]

Today, skincare products containing lead and mercury are illegal. A popular skin-lightening ingredient is hydroquinone. In the United States, products containing hydroquinone (at a maximum of 2 percent of the content) are available over the counter.[53] Higher percentages are available but only under a doctor's care. Although legal in the United States, hydroquinone still does have harsh side effects. Amina Mire explains,

> In the initial phase of skin-bleaching, hydroquinone, by inhibiting the production of melanin, makes the skin appear lighter. However, after 6 months or so of continuous use, hydroquinone chemical deposits penetrate the epidermal layer of the skin and accumulate in the dermal and the subcutaneous layers of the skin, causing irreversible damage to the connective, collagen, fibroblast and cartilage tissues. At this stage, the bleached area of the skin starts getting darker. In addition, the affected area appears as though sprayed with strong blue-black spots. These are complex deposits containing hydroquinone residues and damaged skin tissues. Upon proper clinical and histological examinations, the skin manifests the negative effects of chronic hydroquinone poisoning, such as dermal colloid degeneration, the formation of a glue-like substance, and colloid milium-hydroquinone complex polymers that result, in most cases, in a permanent skin atrophy.[54]

In short, hydroquinone products may work initially. However, prolonged use can cause serious damage to the skin, making these areas look like black and blue spots. At worst, chronic hydroquinone poisoning can cause skin atrophy. Hydroquinone also makes the skin light sensitive, so it is imperative to use a sunscreen. If one fails to use a sunscreen, one is putting oneself at risk for increased sun damage and, in extreme cases, skin cancer. This happens because hydroquinone kills melanin in skin and melanin is what helps protect the skin from ultraviolet sun rays.[55] Other ingredients that are used to help lighten or brighten the skin are retinol, vitamin C, glycolic acid, and herbs, such as licorice root and azalec. Although some specific ingredients have been banned and others are available but are supposed to be used with specific precautions, governments have not thoroughly enforced the ban on mercury or high dosages of hydroquinone in skin care products. Many of the companies that make skin lighteners using these ingredients are outside the United States. The products are often smuggled in.

In 1996, more than 400 Mexican American women and men living in Arizona, California, New Mexico, and Texas got mercury poisoning after using a skin-bleaching cream called Creme de Belleza-Manning made in Mexico and imported to the United States illegally. Creme de Belleza-Manning contains roughly 15 percent by weight of mercury chloride or calomel.[56]

In another instance, in Hong Kong, there was an investigation regarding skincare companies that still use mercury in their products in the 2000s. Although most of the sellers said they did not realize that the products had mercury in them, one supplier told an investigator, "What is wrong with a little mercury in the cream, as long as it can make ladies beautiful?"[57] For some, like the woman with whose story this chapter began, the quest to lighten one's skin rivals that of someone who is addicted to drugs. Even with these side effects, some women are still willing to seek out such products through illegal means and will put their health at risk in search of an idea of beauty that they have been sold.

NOTES

1. Joanne Rondilla wrote this chapter with research help from Lilynda Agvateesiri.

2. Margie Quimpo-Espino, "Can her face launch P1B worth of sales?" *Philippine Daily Inquirer* (July 27, 2003).

3. Linda Collard, "Asian Women in Pursuit of White Skin," Synovate, http://www.marketfacts.com/en/news/press_details.php?id=53 (accessed on December 15, 2004).

4. Ronald Takaki, *Iron Cages: Race and Culture in 19th Century America* (Seattle: University of Washington Press, 1988), 5.

5. Takaki, *Iron Cages.*

6. Takaki, *Iron Cages,* 32–34.

7. Michael Omi and Howard Winant, *Racial Formation in the United States: From the 1960s to the 1990s* (New York: Routeledge, 1994), 55.

8. Omi and Winant, *Racial Formation in the United States,* 55–56.

9. George Lipsitz, *The Possessive Investment in Whiteness: How White People Profit from Identity Politics* (Philadelphia: Temple University Press, 1998), vii.

10. From a print advertisement for: *L'Oreal's ReNoviste* and *Nivea Day Cream, Crest Whitening Strips* commercial, www.avreskinscare.com/skin_menu.html, www.skinbleaching.net.

11. Wendy Chapkis, *Beauty Secrets: Women and the Politics of Appearance* (Boston: South End Press, 1986), 37. Although many may argue that in the U.S. advertising is becoming more diverse with its vast array of representatives, actors, and actresses in the media, coupled with the endless varieties of products that are ethnic specific, we urge people to take a second look.

12. Kathy Peiss, *Hope in a Jar: The Making of America's Beauty Culture* (New York: Metropolitan Books, 1998), 41.

13. Peiss, *Hope in a Jar*, 32.

14. Peiss, *Hope in a Jar*, 41.

15. Peiss, *Hope in a Jar*, 35, 42.

16. Peiss, *Hope in a Jar*, 42–43.

17. For example, in all of the mentioned images, the Asian female is portrayed as a prostitute (as in *Miss Saigon*) or the White hero's decoration (as in the James Bond film). The Asian male, on the other hand, is seen as a dangerous yet asexual martial artist (just check out any Jackie Chan film) or a school nerd (William Hung). All of these portrayals are Eurocentric constructions of what Asians are supposed to be.

18. Patricia Hill-Collins, *Black Feminist Thought: Knowledge, Consciousness and the Politics of Empowerment* (New York: Routledge, 2000), 69.

19. Lipsitz, *Possessive Investment*, 1.

20. Susan Bordo, *Unbearable Weight: Feminism, Western Culture and the Body*. (Berkeley: University of California Press, 2003).

21. *New Beauty* and *Skin* are magazines that focus primarily on topics related to plastic surgery and major skincare procedures. Mark Magnier, "If You've Bought it, Flaunt it," *Los Angeles Times* (August 21, 2004).

22. Chapkis, *Beauty Secrets*, 76.

23. Shiseido and Shu Uemura are available in free-standing boutiques or in fine department stores. Esolis, DHC, Pola are all Japan-based direct sales companies whose products are available online, via mail-order catalogs, or through independent sales representatives.

24. *Esolis* catalog, March 2003, p. 2.

25. Peiss, *Hope in a Jar*.

26. Although we are using the Philippines as an example, similar observations can be made about other parts of Asia.

27. Here, we would like to point out that tan skin (especially skin that looks like it has been enhanced either through natural time in the sun or through some type of tanning process) is a marker of leisure and is temporary. If someone is naturally dark skinned, then the racial meanings are different. Naturally dark skin points toward a more permanent social difference presumed to be linked to one's genes.

28. Deborah Root, *Cannibal Culture: Art, Appropriation, and the Commodification of Difference* (Boulder, CO: Westview Press, 1998), 130.

29. From Philippine advertisements for: *SkinWhite*, *L'Oreal Plentitude White Perfect*, *Armada* sunscreen, *L'Oreal White Perfect Mask*. From a Canadian cosmetics company: www.skinlightening.com, www.revivalabs.com/skinlightening.htm.

30. For example, when walking through a cosmetics department store, it feels like many of the salespeople were recruited directly from the nearest modeling agency. Granted, not everyone behind the counter is modelesque, but companies do pay attention to one's looks when hiring their sales representatives.

31. Lilynda Agvateesiri, "Marketing Whiteness in Thailand." Student paper.

32. Mia Tuan, *Forever Foreigners or Honorary Whites?: The Asian Ethnic Experience Today* (New Brunswick: Rutgers University Press, 1999); Eduardo Bonilla-Silva and David G. Embrick, "Black, Honorary White, and White: The Future of Race in the United States?" in *Mixed Messages*, ed. David L. Brunsma (Boulder, CO: Lynne

Rienner, 2006), 33–48; Keith Osajima, "Asian Americans as the Model Minority: An Analysis of the Popular Press Image in the 1960s and 1980s," in *Reflections on Shattered Windows: Promises and Prospects for Asian American Studies*, ed. Gary Y. Okihiro (Pullman: Washington State University Press, 1998), 165–74; Lucie Cheng and Philip Q. Yang, "The 'Model Minority' Deconstructed," in *Ethnic Los Angeles*, ed. Roger Waldinger and Mehdi Bozorgmehr (New York: Russell Sage Foundation, 1996), 305–44; Won Moo Hurh and Kwang Chung Kim, "The Success Image of Asian Americans," *Ethnic and Racial Studies* 12 (1984): 512–38; Stacey J. Lee, *Unraveling the "Model Minority" Stereotype* (New York: Teachers College, Columbia University, 1996); Vivian S. Louie, *Compelled to Excel: Immigration, Education, and Opportunity among Chinese Americans* (Calif.: Stanford University Press, 2004).

33. Margaret L. Hunter, *Race, Gender, and the Politics of Skin Tone* (New York: Routledge, 2005), 57.

34. Judith Williamson, "Woman Is an Island: Femininity and Colonization," in *Studies in Entertainment*, ed. Tania Modleski (Bloomington and Indianapolis: Indiana University Press, 1986), 101.

35. Collard, "Asian Women in Pursuit of White Skin."

36. Hunter, *Politics of Skin Tone*, 70–71.

37. Similar dynamics work in Cambodia where a relatively dark-skinned local population has mixed to some degree with lighter-skinned Chinese, Vietnamese, or French, with a hierarchy of light over dark also being formed.

38. *Esolis* catalog, p. 8.

39. Mire, "Skin Bleaching."

40. Morena refers to some one who is darker skinned, while mestiza refers to someone who is lighter-skinned and mixed race.

41. Lora Gahol, "Whiteners Won't Transform 'Morena' into 'Mestiza,'" *Philippine Daily Inquirer* (April 30, 2003).

42. In later versions of this catalog, this model's photograph was removed completely. Although we cannot give definite answers as to why this was done, one has to wonder why her photograph was positioned in this particular section and why her image was erased from later catalogs.

43. Catherine Lutz and Jane L. Collins, *Reading National Geographic* (Chicago: University of Chicago Press, 1993), 56.

44. Miriam Jordan, "Creams for a Lighter Skin Capture the Asian Market; Especially in India Fair Color as a Cultural Virtue," *International Herald Tribune* (April 24, 1998).

45. Root, *Cannibal Culture*, 9.

46. Williamson, "Woman Is an Island," 116.

47. Peiss, *Hope in a Jar*, 146.

48. Peiss, *Hope in a Jar*, 223.

49. Peiss, *Hope in a Jar*

50. Russell, et al., *Color Complex*, 49–50.

51. Peiss, *Hope in a Jar*, 21–22.

52. Compiled by the Consumer Council of Hong Kong, the Hong Kong Department of Health, and a number of Hong Kong dermatologists. "Creams with mercury

are unsafe. Heavy metals such as mercury can enter the body and stay on as a poison, affecting the bones, nervous tissue, and blood-forming system," CNN, http://www.cnn.com/2002/WORLD/asiapcf/east/05/14/asia.mercury/index.html (accessed on December 1, 2003).

53. In August 2006, the FDA announced plans to ban hydroquinone because of possible health risks. The ban sparked an outcry by numerous cosmetics companies and skincare professionals. A final FDA decision is due in spring 2007.

54. Mire, "Skin Bleaching."

55. Mire, "Skin Bleaching."

56. Mire, "Skin Bleaching."

57. Marianne Bray, "Skin Deep: Dying to be White," CNN, http://edition.cnn.com2002/WORLD/asiapcf/east/05/13/asia.whitening, (accessed on December 1, 2003).

The Unkindest Cut:
Cosmetic Surgery[1]

It is with this sense of joy and anticipation that I decided to publish this magazine, *skin.*; to share with you the wealth of knowledge I am constantly gathering! Hopefully these articles will equip YOU with the knowledge YOU need to help you with your beauty choices. What YOU are today is the sum total of your choice. What I am today is the sum total of all my choices. It was only after I had chosen to fix my outer self, that I was able to start working on my inner self. After this, I woke up to LIFE AND ALL OF ITS POSSIBILITIES, achieving my goal of living the best way I could live. It's a wonderful feeling! So here and now, let's all choose to discover HOW BEAUTIFUL LIFE IS and most especially, HOW BEAUTIFUL WE ALL ARE in our own—SKIN!

—Dr. Vicki Belo,
plastic surgeon and Editor-in-Chief of *skin.* magazine[2]

We want to show there is no difference between natural and artificial beauty. Cosmetic surgery is the way of the future. Like exercise and diet, it is just another means of self-improvement that gives everyone the opportunity to be more beautiful.

—Han Wei,
organizer of China's first Miss Plastic Surgery pageant[3]

Men and women of Asian lineage seek cosmetic eyelid surgery for the same fundamental reason as their Occidental counterparts, namely, to feel better about themselves. While enhancing the existing eyelid structure so that it better conforms to widely-accepted norms of aesthetics and balance is indeed a major goal, feeling happier and more confident is yet another.

—Asian Eyelid Surgery: An Overview, drmeronk.com [4]

*T*his book is primarily about the colorism phenomenon in Asian American families and communities. Cosmetic surgery—buying the fruits of a surgeon's skills to change one's features in the attempt to be more beautiful (and, we would argue, to look more White)—is not the same thing as yearning after white skin. Yet it seems obvious that there are connections between these two phenomena. Accordingly, we will devote this shorter chapter to a consideration of Asian Americans' consumption of cosmetic surgery.

In 2004 alone, Americans spent approximately $9 billion on cosmetic surgery. The top five surgical procedures of preference were: liposuction, nose reshaping (rhinoplasty), breast augmentation, eyelid surgery (blepharoplasty), and facelifts. Non-Whites were 15 percent of those going under the knife. In 2003, the top surgeries for Asian Americans were blepharoplasty followed by rhinoplasty.[5] While these figures account for surgery in the United States, cosmetic surgery is popular all over the world. In China, cosmetic surgery is a $2.4 billion industry and is growing at a rate of 20 percent per year. In 2004, China hosted its first Miss Plastic Surgery contest, "the world's first pageant for artificial beauties," and promised to revisit the pageant annually.[6] That same year, the Philippine-based Belo Medical Group (BMG) and the Department of Tourism (DOT) announced plans to launch "Belo Beauty Vacation," which invites people from Europe and America to indulge in luxurious vacations while getting cosmetic surgery by highly trained professionals, at a rate that is cheaper than in their own native countries.[7]

For many, cosmetic surgery is a way for one to reinvent oneself from the outside in. As Dr. Vicki Belo asserts, being beautiful on the outside leads a woman (and it is mainly women) to work on her beauty on the inside, because one cannot exist without the other. Han Wei, organizer of China's Miss Plastic Surgery contest, embraces this idea by comparing cosmetic surgery to diet and exercise—it is something that people do to survive and thrive in today's world. The technology is there, so why not use it? Many proponents of cosmetic surgery, such as Belo and Wei, firmly believe that when all is said and done, the decision to have surgery is ultimately about feeling good about oneself. According to many surgeons, cosmetic surgery allows people to take control and claim the beauty that lies beneath the skin.

While this may be true for some, this chapter explores an alternative view by asking, are people really taking control of their beauty or are they being controlled by such standards? When one does undergo surgery, does one's life really change? What are the racialized implications behind the popularity of plastic surgery? Although in the United States non-Whites receive only 15 percent of cosmetic surgeries, it is important to explore such questions, because cosmetic surgery is a global phenomenon that has impact on all communities of color in the United States, including Asian Americans.

Additionally, whereas non-Whites are a small percentage of those going under the knife in the United States, statistics do not account for those who travel overseas to undergo surgery. Nor do the figures include those who have surgery performed by people who are not board certified. This chapter will explore these questions by first looking at a brief history of cosmetic surgery in the United States. Then, by way of example, we will connect aspects of this history to a Southern California-based clinic's extensive advertisement for eyelid surgery. We will also look at the developing beauty tourist industry in the Philippines. The chapter will end by examining some of the dangers of cosmetic surgery, which many of its proponents are unwilling to discuss.

UNNECESSARY SURGERY

Plastic surgery can be traced as far back as 600 B.C. in India, where surgeons altered the nose by taking a part of the cheek and attaching it to the tip of the nose. Italy's Gasparo Tagliacozzi is considered to be the "father of modern plastic surgery" because, in the late 1580s, he was known to restore the noses of men who had been involved in street brawls. Tagliacozzi did this by transferring skin from the upper arm to the nose.[8] In its origins, plastic surgery was not intended to enhance one's beauty. Plastic surgery was originally intended to treat severe damage and deformities. World War I and modern warfare gave rise to much more widespread use of plastic surgery, because patients, such as soldiers, who were wounded in combat were prime targets for the more reputable plastic surgeons. These surgeons believed that a soldier who underwent facial reconstruction needed the surgery to regain his prewar lifestyle. People who had plastic surgery did it out of necessity. As a medical practice, plastic surgery was seen to heal patients.[9]

On the other hand, cosmetic or beauty surgery was not considered a reputable field, because surgeons and the public alike believed that undergoing cosmetic surgery for vanity put healthy people at unnecessary risk of health complications. Early on, many patients were rejected from undergoing surgery when surgeons felt the procedure was unnecessary. This was the main difference between plastic surgery and cosmetic surgery—plastic surgery was born out of necessity and cosmetic surgery was deemed more superficial. Also, the American public believed that physical traits, such as a large nose or small breasts, were simple facts of life and that one's character was determined by a person's attitude and not necessarily her or his appearance.[10]

Cosmetic surgery's negative reputation began to shift for several reasons. First, the shift in the locus of the American population from country to city over the first half of the twentieth century affected ideas about cosmetic surgery; urban identity was based more on public self-presentation than on local or familial relationships. Also, by the 1920s and 1930s, Americans started to believe that one's looks had economic value and were important to social success as well as to one's mental health. This became particularly significant during the Depression. When jobs were scarce, many believed that one's appearance defined one's drive and determination. Looking good helped people gain employment in an ultra-competitive job market.[11]

In the post-World War II era, cosmetic surgery was primarily targeted to middle-class, middle-aged White women. This was because American culture began to shift focus and valorize beauty, which many equated with youth. Women were targeted because many believed that women aged faster than men because they were supposed to be more emotional. Additionally, it was not acceptable for men to have cosmetic surgery unless the circumstances were extreme (such as the solider whose face or body was deformed). For men, age made them look distinctive and even distinguished. To go under the knife meant that they were vain (and that vanity often labeled them as homosexual). Also, the surgical techniques used in those years made it difficult for men to hide the scarring. For women, it seemed natural for them to need cosmetic surgery to keep up particular standards of beauty. This is why they were primarily targeted for the procedures and why women getting surgery was more socially acceptable.[12]

Although the number of men getting cosmetic surgery today is slowly rising, the percentage of men is much smaller than that of women. In 1998, for example, men made up only 10 percent of the cosmetic surgery procedures in the United States. The only area where they outnumbered women was in hair transplants: men were 83 percent of those surgeries. In 2003, 334,000 men had Botox injections compared to the 2.56 million women who had such injections.[13] The difference in numbers is also indicative of how we perceive men's and women's relationships to plastic surgery. Today, when men go under the knife, it is assumed that they do it for functional (and therefore legitimate) purposes. Plastic surgery for men has less to do with vanity and more to do with economic gain. According to Kathy Davis, "Men seek out plastic surgery for 'functional reasons' or 'clear-cut physical complaints.'"[14]

On the other hand, when a woman goes under the knife, it is assumed that she must have flaws she needs to correct. The need for a woman to correct her flaws is seen as natural as opposed to functional. Davis notes, "Since medicine has historically defined the female body as deficient and in need of repair, cosmetic surgery is easily legitimated as 'natural' and, therefore, acceptable therapy for women's problems with their appearance."[15] This is why cosmetic surgery marketing is targeted at women. It is because it is seen as natural and therefore acceptable for a woman to want to alter her appearance and "fix" her flaws. The idea is so ingrained that when a woman has no desire to go under the knife, she is sometimes even seen as abnormal. It is similar to targeting skin lightening products in colonized countries, such as the Philippines. Normalizing the idea of having the option of fixing one's perceived flaws opens the doors to big business.

NOT TRYING TO BE WHITE

With respect to Asians and Asian Americans, going under the knife has a distinct set of implications. It seems that, regardless of gender, when Asians and Asian Americans undergo surgery, they do it out of motives that may be interpreted as either necessity or vanity, depending on one's perspective. For example, when an Asian woman gets eyelid surgery, she may say that she went through the procedure to have a more natural-looking double eyelid, to look more awake or to make eye makeup application easier.[16] On the surface, these reasons may seem vain. However, she sees them as necessary. The "necessity" of these surgeries is connected to racist notions of how Asians and Asian Americans should look; that is, it is determined by what Asians should look like in the White imagination.

A catch phrase that is commonly used when referring to eyelid surgery is "ethnic correction."[17] Doctors will use this and other similar phrases to justify why Asian and Asian American patients should go under the knife. However, what is ethnic correctness? What is it about one's ethnicity that cosmetic surgery aims to correct? Why does this industry continue to use the racist implications behind the idea of correcting one's ethnicity to profit? As mentioned in chapter 4, the idea of ethnic correctness is related to Benjamin Rush's notion of curing the disease of Black skin. Instead of focusing on correcting skin color, as in the case of skin bleaches, cosmetic surgery has found its way to curing the disease of ethnic features. Sadly, this is not a new phenomenon, as the earliest recorded case of a patient altering his features for racial reasons dates back to the mid-1920s.

In 1926, a Japanese man named Shima Kito underwent cosmetic surgery to remove the slant in his eyes. He also had a nose job and his lower lip was tightened. Kito did this because he wanted to marry his White girlfriend, Mildred Ross from Iowa. While they loved each other, Ross knew her parents would not approve of the interracial match. Therefore, Kito went under the knife in the hope that Ross's parents would approve of him and their marriage despite his Japanese heritage. After the surgery, Kito and Ross were engaged and Kito stated that he would complete his transformation by changing his name to William White.[18]

Asians and Asian Americans have a unique relationship to cosmetic surgery, because early on, many Asians (such as Shima Kito) used surgery as a means to erase their Asian features to adopt a more Westernized look. Currently, the most popular procedure among Asian Americans is eyelid surgery (blepharoplasty), followed by nose jobs (rhinoplasty). In the United States population as a whole, the top surgeries are liposuction, breast augmentation, and eyelid surgery (in that order).[19] It seems that the surgeries Asians choose are designed to alter traits that are distinctly Asian—the eyes and the nose. "While the features that white women primarily seek to alter through cosmetic surgery do not correspond to conventional markers of racial identity, those features that Asian American women primarily seek to alter do correspond with such markers."[20]

Nonetheless, many who do undergo surgery claim that they have no desire to be White. Korean American plastic surgeon Dr. Marc Yune states, "I've never had a patient come in and specifically say, 'I want to look Caucasian.' In fact, they specifically say, 'I don't want an American eye, I don't want a round eye.'"[21] Beijing-based cosmetic surgeon Dr. Fushin Ma says, "I don't think they deliberately want to copy the West, they just believe these features look prettier. It's modern fashion."[22]

There seems to be a discrepancy about why Asians are going under the knife. If Asian women are happy with their distinctly Asian features, then why are many of them choosing to alter these traits? According to the website of California-based eyelid surgeon Dr. Frank Meronk, the reasons for changing distinctly Asian features are:

> Irrespective of ethnicity, an upper eyelid is typically considered more attractive by most people if it lacks excessive skin and fat, possesses a reasonably defined crease (which makes the eye appear bigger—a universal signal of youth and attention), and displays at least some platform of exposed skin between the crease and the eyelashes (which, in ladies, allows for a more effective application of makeup). A well-contoured lower eyelid free of bulging fat projects an image of youth, energy, and rest. While all so-called 'standards' of physical beauty are culturally variable and dependent upon the eye of the beholder, most experienced eyelid surgeons agree that the qualities noted here are generally appreciated across many diverse cultures and not solely a matter of Western bias.[23]

This rhetoric avoids any racialized meaning behind the undesirability of a single eyelid by explaining it in medical terms. Instead of describing an eye that has a single-fold or Asian eyelid, that same eye is described as having excessive skin and fat. The site also states that a double-lidded eye makes one look more awake and allows for easier makeup application (as if makeup application were a medically sound tool to achieve health). In a series of interviews with cosmetic surgeons, Regina Kaw observes, "All of the doctors in my study stated that a 'practical' benefit for Asian American women undergoing surgery to create or enlarge their eyelid folds is that they can put eye make-up on more appropriately."[24] Kaw also asserts:

> According to my Asian American informants who had undergone cosmetic surgery, their plastic surgeons used several medical terms to problematize the shape of their eyes so as to define it as a medical condition. For instance, many patients were told that they had "excess fat" on their eyelids and it was "normal" for them to feel dissatisfied with they way they looked. "Lots of Asians have the same puffiness over the eyelid, and they often feel better about themselves after the operation," doctors would assure their Asian American patients.[25]

By framing a single eyelid as a medical flaw, surgeons successfully convince patients that they are doing the right thing by going through the surgery. They also dodge the larger racialized implications by masking them with the idea that a double eyelid will make the patient feel better and improve her overall mental well-being.

The doctors' description also tries to save itself from racial meanings by explaining that beauty standards exist in every culture and that what constitutes an attractive eyelid is defined by many cultures, not by Western bias. Again, Kaw answers this assumption by asserting, "Ignoring the fact that the Asian American women's decision to undergo cosmetic surgery has anything to do with the larger society's racial prejudice, the doctors state that their Asian American women patients come to cosmetic surgeons to mold their own standards of beauty."[26] Apparently, those beauty standards generated by Asian women just happen to coincide with the way they perceive White women to look.

Ironically, while Dr. Meronk's site states that definitions of an attractive eyelid have nothing to do with Western bias, it goes on to explain why Asian eyes in particular are of special concern for a blepharoplasty specialist, such as himself. The site does this by explaining that Asian eyelids are different from White eyelids:

> Men and women of Asian lineage seek cosmetic eyelid surgery for the same fundamental reason as their Occidental counterparts, namely, to feel better about themselves. . . . While approximately half of all Asian people are born with an upper eyelid crease, that crease is different from an Occidental crease in important ways, most notably in height, shape and depth.[27]

The comparison alone automatically refutes the initial assertion that getting eyelid surgery has nothing to do with Westernized standards of beauty. In fact, it has everything to do with such beauty standards. Another section of the website, "How Asian and Occidental Eyelids Differ," complete with a color-coded guide, gives an elaborate biological explanation of how Asian and European eyelids differ.[28]

Finally, the Meronk site attempts to explain the special circumstances of people who are of mixed racial descent. Crudely, it states that people who are of Asian and White descent typically undergo surgery, because their Asian features are hiding their White features.

> Patients of mixed Asian and Occidental heritage demonstrate great variability in upper lid structure and crease appearance. For instance, some show extremely well-defined creases inherited from the Occidental parent that sit "hidden" beneath the thicker soft tissues inherited from the Asian parent. In such patients, cosmetic eye surgery may be undertaken solely to better expose the crease.[29]

In short, even mixed-race patients (described as part Asian and part "Occidental") have to undergo surgery, because in some unfortunate instances, the Asian traits surface before the White traits. Luckily, such a patient is part White, and with the miracle of cosmetic surgery, one can correct the person's racial appearance by erasing the Asian part. Although an outrageous claim, we must remember that this comes from a highly trained medical professional. The rhetoric uses pseudo-scientific jargon in an attempt to make what sounds like a valid and medically sound claim. It is imperative that we see through this carefully and critically, because these claims have nothing to do with mental health concerns for a patient's longing to be beautiful. Presumably, in such a case, psychotherapy centered on the beauty issue and the person's racial identity would be an appropriate alternative intervention. Rather, this rhetoric has to do with the growing business of cosmetic surgery and how it profits from the idea of ethnic correction. Even when doctors feel that there is nothing wrong with patients, they still will have them undergo procedures.[30]

BEAUTY TOURISM: NOSE JOBS BY THE BEACH

Modern plastic surgery was rooted in the late nineteenth century and made its way around the globe following the paths of the colonial expansion of capitalism. The earliest known Japanese procedure was eyelid surgery performed in 1896 by Dr. K. Mikamo. In the Philippines, American surgeons noted similar surgery in the 1950s.[31] While cosmetic surgery probably existed in various parts of Asia before colonial influence, the overwhelming popularity of cosmetic surgery happened in part because of colonialism.[32] During the colonization of different parts of Asia, Americans brought various types of media imagery, which local populations would internalize. This would then prompt many people, particularly women, to opt for surgery. Elizabeth Haiken points out this relationship in Vietnam. She notes:

> The escalation of American involvement in Vietnam extended Americanized visual culture farther around the globe. As well as internalized standards of female beauty, American GIs brought with them external representations in the form of *Playboy* magazines and pin-up posters. In what observers insisted was not a coincidence, more and more Vietnamese women began to seek plastic surgery.[33]

Over time, an interesting shift has occurred. A growing beauty tourist industry (sometimes referred to as "medical tourism") has emerged. People from Europe and America are traveling to colonized nations to have cosmetic surgery performed. No, they are not going to Asia to obtain Asian features. Instead, they are taking advantage of the low cost of surgery while indulging in a top-of-the-line vacation package for their period of recovery.[34]

In 2004, the BMG, one of the Philippines' premiere plastic surgery clinics, along with the DOT, announced plans for the Belo Beauty Vacation. Targeting American and European clientele, the marriage between BMG and DOT aims to make the Philippines a leader in medical tourism. Vacation packages include cosmetic surgery and a stay at a premiere luxury resort for recovery. Representatives from BMG claim:

> The Philippines, and other Asian countries, are fast becoming the global centers for medical tourism. Based on records, doctors here have performed more complex cosmetic surgery than many of their European and U.S. counterparts. The success of Belo Medical Group stems from a tremendously high investment that we do through constant training, expensive and up-to-date technology, methods and equipment. [35]

Clients can get surgery using the best technology by highly skilled doctors who were most likely trained in the United States or Europe, and they can save an average of 30 to 70 percent of the cost that is charged by clinics in their native countries. These packages are especially enticing because of the positive reputation of Philippine surgeons. In her testimonial, Stephanie, an African American client of the BMG, had liposuction. She had an American doctor examine her when she got back from the Philippines, and the doctor claimed her surgery was top notch. This convinced her to go back to the Philippines to have warts removed and breast augmentation.[36] Testimonials like these are the cornerstone of BMG marketing.

The success of this project also relates to colonialism abroad. Many of the doctors in the Philippines were trained in the United States or Europe. They know English and understand American and European culture. These factors put patients at ease and encourage them to feel confident in traveling to the Philippines to have surgery. The Philippines option also allows plastic surgery to be affordable to the masses, at the same time it introduces the Philippines as a hot vacation destination. Prospects for the BMG and DOT projects are good.

Other countries, such as the Dominican Republic, have cashed in on the multimillion dollar medical tourism industry: 80 percent of their patients come from abroad. The growing interest in medical tourism abroad has caused concern among American doctors. In 1999, Dr. Edgar Contreras from the Dominican Republic was charged with two counts of involuntary homicide after patients died under his care.[37] Stories, such as this, have made headlines in the United States. While it may be important for people to be aware of the possibility of malpractice in surgery administered abroad, American surgeons also injure their patients on occasion. What these American surgeons are touting as ethical concerns are really mainly business concerns.

Finally, the low cost of these beauty tourist packages makes cosmetic surgery accessible to a greater number of people than ever before. What used to be available only to the wealthy and the upper middle class can now be obtained by virtually anybody. For Asian Americans, this gives them a chance to go home, get surgery, visit family, and return with what they regard as improved features.

DYING TO BE BEAUTIFUL

An MTV show called *I Want a Famous Face* purports to show real-life plastic surgery cases. One episode featured a young woman named Sha (pronounced Shay) who wanted to look like her idol, Pamela Anderson. The show focused mainly on Sha and the process of getting breast augmentation. In the end, it showed her celebrating her new body because, as with most reality TV, there always has to be a happy ending. However, all but lost in the middle of the episode was a short, hardly noticeable segment about a different woman who underwent surgery and ended up regretting it (this second woman will be called Jane). Like Sha, Jane aspired to be a *Playboy* model. In a feeble attempt to show both the good and the bad of cosmetic surgery, MTV presented Jane's story as a brief alternative narrative. Jane shared her experiences of re-jection from modeling because her body looked unnatural, the implants were too large for her frame, and they ended up rippling, which made her breasts look lumpy.

Most programming—and certainly all advertising—about plastic sur-gery does not show the dangerous side of the practice. While the ads show that many patients will attest that their surgeries helped them feel better about themselves, there are also others who regret ever going under the knife. The darker aftermath is prolonged health problems. Often a person realizes that, even after surgery, she or he still did not gain the self-confidence that she or he was expecting. Some of the negative physical side effects possible in plastic surgery are as follows:

- Bleeding and hematoma (although postoperation bleeding is natural, excessive bleeding can be dangerous);
- Infection (the body is most susceptible to infection seventy-two hours after surgery);
- Seroma (fluid collection that happens when the skin has been separated; this is most common in procedures such as tummy tucks);
- Suture reactions (as foreign objects to the body, sutures can be rejected and the body can push them out; if untreated or unnoticed, the area can get a serious infection);
- Skin reactions;
- Wound separation;
- Necrosis (tissue death caused by a lack of oxygen);
- Nerve damage (this can cause muscle weakness or paralysis).[38]

There is, however, another side to the danger of cosmetic surgery, and that deals with the psychological and emotional side of the pressure to maintain a specific beauty standard. In "A Letter to My Sister," Lisa Park writes to her sister who committed suicide. In her sister's moments of depression, it was suggested that she try to reinvent herself. Park explains:

> One of the ways you tried to affirm your "new" resolve was to change your physical appearance through plastic surgery, for which our parents willingly put up the money in a effort to keep you happy. . . . Your obsession with plastic surgery exposed the myth of the whole beauty industry, which portrays plastic surgery as a beautifying, renewing experience, "something special you do just for you." . . . Help is a four-letter word. You decided death was your only alternative to being stuck with an inescapable body. As soon as you were released from the hospital, you committed yourself to finding a way to kill yourself. Now, on top of what you considered a mistake of a body, you wanted to avoid being thrown into a mental institution, where you were sure you were headed as a consequence of being found out by psychiatrists.[39]

In an honest exploration of her sister's death, Park illustrates the relationship many Asian American women have with cosmetic surgery. On one hand, the industry convinces individuals that surgery is a good thing, because feeling beautiful can change one's outlook on life. However, no amount of cosmetic surgery can erase the historical, political, social, and economic injustice that Asian Americans experience on a daily basis. After the surgery was performed, Park's sister was still an Asian American woman living in a world where a woman's racial and ethnic identity defined who she was and how she would be treated. Cosmetic surgery did not change her income level. It did not change her community's lack of representation in the media and politics. Nor did it change the way this Asian American woman saw herself in the American landscape. Park notes that her sister's depression was caused because she was an outcast. She rebelled against the model minority myth:

> Our inclusion into the American process turned out to be our worst form of oppression. Most people are proud to call themselves Americans, but why would you want to become a productive, well-adjusted citizen when the primary requisite of American-ness is racism? Isn't our madness often the only evidence we have at all to show for this civilizing terror? . . . We became pathetic victims of whiteness. We permed our hair and could afford to buy trendy clothes. Money, at least, gave us some material status. But we knew we could never become 'popular,' in other words, accepted. It had something to do with our 'almond-shaped' eyes, but we never called it racism. You once asked, 'What's wrong with trying to be white?' You said your way of dealing with racism was not to let them know it bothered you. But they don't want it to bother us. If it did, they would have a revolution on their hands. The 'just-convince-them-they-should-be-like-us' tactic. It is so important for the American racial hierarchy to keep us consuming its ideals so that we attack ourselves instead of the racial neuroses it manufactures.[40]

The last few lines of this excerpt remind us what is at the heart of the cosmetic surgery industry. It has nothing to do with a patient's well-being. Rather, when it is marketed to Asian American women, it is more concerned with maintaining a racialized hierarchy and making a profit.

These snippets of the Park sisters' story illustrate the pressure to participate in damaging beauty practices, such as cosmetic surgery. They also show the power and privilege in Whiteness and the position Asian Americans hold as sometimes honorary Whites.[41] We cannot change our race, but supposedly we can change our bodies so that we can nearly attain a White standard of beauty. The lure of plastic surgery and other beauty-related technologies fools us into believing this. However, Park's story about her sister shows us that beauty practices, such as cosmetic surgery, do not automatically make one's life better. This is because the problem does not lie solely within oneself. Kathy Davis explains,

Cosmetic surgery cannot be understood as a matter of individual choice, nor is it an artifact of consumer culture which, in principle, affects us all. On the contrary, cosmetic surgery has to be situated in the context of how gender/power is exercised in late modern western culture. Cosmetic surgery belongs to a broad regime of technologies, practices and discourses, which define the female body as deficient and in need of constant transformation.[42]

Asian American women inhabit a marginal position as members of a model minority who are socially acceptable but not quite White. For some of them, cosmetic surgery presents itself as a way to try to jump the racial gap. Some of those are successful in their own eyes. Others, like Lisa Park's sister, are not.

NOTES

1. A draft of this chapter was prepared by Joanne Rondilla, with research assistance by Sara Cruz and Christie Trieu. Joanne Rondilla wrote the final manuscript.

2. Vicki Belo, "Editor's Note," *skin. Magazine* (2004), 6.

3. Abigail Haworth, "Nothing about These Women is Real," *Marie Claire* (July 2005): 60.

4. "Asian Eyelid Surgery: An Overview," *Meronk Blepharoplasty Eyelid Surgery for California,* http://drmeronk.com/asian/asian-overview.html (accessed on October 20, 2003).

5. "Cosmetic Enhancement Statistics at a Glance," *New Beauty* (Summer-Fall 2005): 25; Anna M. Park, "Cutting Through the Plastic," *Audrey* (April/May 2005): 44-46.

6. Haworth, "Nothing About These Women," 60.

7. "Beauty Trip," *skin* (2004): 41–42.

8. Elizabeth Haiken, *Venus Envy: The History of Cosmetic Surgery* (Baltimore: Johns Hopkins University Press, 1997), 4–5.

9. Haiken, *Venus Envy*, 93.

10. Haiken, *Venus Envy*, 4–5, 93.

11. Haiken, *Venus Envy*, 105–107.

12. Haiken, *Venus Envy*, 132, 150; Kathy Davis, "A 'Dubious Equality': Men, Women and Cosmetic Surgery," *Body and Society* 8, no. 1 (2002): 58.

13. Davis, 50; William McCall, "Nip, Tuck, Shot . . . More Men are Using Cosmetic Surgery," *Seattle Post Intelligencer* (January 6, 2005).

14. Davis, 55.

15. Davis, 55.

16. Because nearly half of Asians naturally have a double eyelid, those with a monolid are simply seeking to look the way the other half of the Asian population looks.

17. Park, "Cutting Through The Plastic," 47.

18. Haiken, *Venus Envy*, 200.

19. Park, "Cutting Through the Plastic," 44–46.

20. Eugenia Kaw, "Medicalization of Racial Features: Asian American Women and Cosmetic Surgery," *Medical Anthropology Quarterly* 7, no. 1 (1993): 75.

21. Christina Valhouli, "Fixing the Asian Eye—Racist or No Big Deal?" Talk Surgery, Inc., November 9, 2001.

22. Haworth, "Nothing About These Women," 62.

23. "Asian Eyelid Surgery: Eyelid Features," *Meronk Blepharoplasty Eyelid Surgery for California*, http://drmeronk.com/asian/asian-eyelid-features.html (accessed on October 20, 2003).

24. Kaw, "Medicalization of Racial Features," 84.

25. Kaw, "Medicalization of Racial Features," 81.

26. Kaw, "Medicalization of Racial Features," 85.

27. "Asian Eyelid Surgery: An Overview."

28. "How Asian and Occidental Eyelids Differ," Meronk Blepharoplasty Eyelid Surgery for California, http://drmeronk.com/asian/asian-eyelid-anatomy.html (accessed on October 20, 2003).

29. "Asian Eyelid Surgery: Asian and Occidental Eyelid Surgery—Differences," *Meronk Blepharoplasty Eyelid Surgery for California*, http://drmeronk.com/asian/asian-overview.html (accessed on October 20, 2003).

30. Kaw, "Medicalization of Racial Features," 83.

31. Sandra L. Gilman, *Creating Beauty to Cure the Soul: Race and Psychology in the Shaping of Aesthetic Surgery* (Durham, N.C.: Duke University Press, 1998), 19; Anna M. Park, "Cutting Through The Plastic," *Audrey* (April/May 2005), 44.

32. We are aware that Japan was never formally colonized by a Western power. Nevertheless, colonial ideas of Western superiority—including the superiority of Western beauty—permeated the country during several periods from the aftermath of the Meiji Restoration to the American occupation of the late 1940s, and on into the twenty-first century.

33. Haiken, *Venus Envy*, 203.

34. This shift would be even more interesting if these Europeans and Americans were traveling to Asia for cosmetic surgery to look Asian as opposed to White. Alas, no such luck. However, this does illustrate the power of colonialism because these overseas doctors specialize both in changing White people's features—a nip here, a tuck there—and in altering the features of Asian clients to give them a White appearance.

35. "Beauty Trip," 42.

36. "Beauty Trip," 41–42.

37. Victoria Corderi, "Plastic Surgery Tourism? Dangers of Going Under the Knife Cheap," *Dateline NBC*, 2005.

38. "Introduction to the Risks of Plastic Surgery," http://www.beautysurg.com/learn/general_risks.html (accessed on June 13, 2005).

39. Lisa Park, "A Letter to My Sister," in *Making More Waves: New Writing by Asian American Women,* edited by Elaine Kim, et al. (Massachusetts: Beacon Press, 1997), 65.

40. Park, "A Letter to My Sister," 57–58.

41. Mia Tuan, *Forever Foreigners or Honorary Whites? The Asian Ethnic Experience Today* (New Brunswick, N.J.: Rutgers University Press, 1998).

42. Davis, "'A Dubious Equality,'" 49.

Epilogue

$\mathscr{A}$t the close of this book we who worked on it want to pause and look back at what we think we have learned about colorism and its effects on Asian Americans. We have listened to the voices of women writers talking about their own lives. We have surveyed a hundred people and asked them pointed questions. We have delved into the murky worlds where skin lighteners and cosmetic surgery are sold and consumed.

It is clear and indisputable that colorism is a phenomenon in every Asian American community, among Filipinos and Thais, Japanese and Chinese, South Asians and Vietnamese, Koreans and Cambodians, and so on. In each of these groups of people, and especially among those who are immigrants, there is a marked preference for lighter skin, for sharper and more pointed features—for oneself, for one's mate, and for one's children. Such desires are especially strong among women and more muted among men, as one would expect with beauty issues.

Some would say (indeed, many of our informants do say) that this longing for lightness is not a longing for Whiteness. That is, they would say that those who want to be lighter are not trying to become White people, but rather they are yearning after old-country, class-derived standards of female beauty, where those who worked did so in the sun, and those with leisure were light of skin. There is a lot of evidence for such longstanding preferences in every Asian country, predating serious contact with Europe or the United States. But it is also possible to argue—indeed, it is essential to understand—that there is a Whiteness move at work here, too, bound up in international celebrity culture and fed by a global capitalist marketing machine. There is particular strength, it seems, when ancient beauty imperatives are overlaid with and reinforced by colonially produced desires.

Whatever the sources of the longing after lightness, it causes a lot of pain. The women whose stories appear in chapter 2 are eloquent in describing the ways that the colors of their skin and the interpretations people write on their features have limited their sense of themselves as competent and attractive people with access to full membership in Asian America. It is worth noting that the issues surrounding color and features are no less fraught for women who are light, and who for that reason may be suspected of ethnic disloyalty by other Asians, than they are for those who are dark and who therefore may be thought of as less beautiful. The interpretation that many people we interviewed laid on Jennifer, the light-skinned woman, of wanton sexuality and dysfunction, together with the stories of rejection told by some of the racially mixed women in chapter 2, suggest that it is not, in fact, better to be light.

Still, the desire for light skin and European features leads many Asian American women to do harmful things to their bodies and spirits. They paint themselves with chemicals that, the advertisers say, will make them beautiful and, some seem to believe, will make them more acceptable, either in White America or among Asian Americans. In fact these products damage their skin, sometimes in terrible ways. Many of the same women and many others opt for cosmetic surgery. Influenced by both Asian and colonial cultural imperatives mediated by skillful advertising, they have themselves sliced and diced in an attempt to reshape their features. Most people who do these things—and most of those who sell the chemicals and the surgical procedures—appeal to some supposed universal beauty norm. We suspect a Whiteness move.

When, however, it comes time for people to choose which of three women—dark, medium, or light—they would most like to be, which they would like to date or marry, and which they would choose for a daughter-in-law, the story is a little different. Universally, the first choice is Jane, the woman of medium tone; she is assumed to be happy, vigorous, and successful. The strong second choice is the dark woman Sarah, whom people associate with virtue, hard work, and family devotion. Jennifer, the light woman, is a poor third, as people write on her features a tale of sexuality, irresponsibility, and inner torment.

This leaves us with a question and a challenge for Asian American women: If women and men in the abstract prefer light skin and pointed features, and if many women succumb to the pressures of advertising and colonial beauty culture to the extent that they will poison their bodies with chemicals and submit to violent surgeries, why then do they prefer the darker woman when it comes to an actual choice? Perhaps this is because regardless of skin color, Asian American women are always seen as the *other*. All the chemical skin lightening products and cosmetic surgery procedures cannot and will not erase one's ethnic identity and all the assumptions that follow it.[1] After all the surgeries and bleaching, the newly created William White will always be Shima Kito.

While we do not doubt that people who do get their skin lightened or go under the knife sometimes achieve their goal of feeling good about themselves or having higher self-esteem, we also recognize that there is a larger force that drives Asian women around the world to alter their bodies. If skin lightening and cosmetic surgery were indeed the answer to raising low self-esteem, then why do women invest in multiple surgeries? Why are women not walking out into the world more happy and confident? Why is it that when a woman fixes one flaw, she usually finds a new one over which to obsess? The beauty industry makes billions of dollars each year on the promise that they will provide the ultimate answers to one's insecurities. However, we must remember that skin lightening and cosmetic surgery are not the solution to a world that profits from inequality. When all is said and done, the beauty industry cannot account for why women feel the need to alter themselves in the first place. Inequalities that are defined by one's ethnic background, gender, class, and skin color are part of an everyday life that is rooted in many years of oppression. A chemical treatment or surgery cannot erase this reality.

People all over the world are investing in skin lightening and cosmetic surgery at alarming rates. By promoting such procedures, tourism has found a new way to make money in third world countries. Sadly, many see these developments as a celebration of the union between medical technology and commerce. However, we must ask, what has this union done to mend poverty or political strife in the countries that host the medical tourism? While some enjoy the convenience of inexpensive beauty surgery, we cannot help but wonder what kind of world we are creating for future generations of Asians across the world. That many Asians undergo surgery to alter the traits that make them distinctly Asian (their skin color, eyes, nose, and body shape) suggests that the beauty industry is complicit in a type of ethnic cleansing that is masked by the rhetoric of feeling good about oneself.

When Joanne Rondilla's nephew was seven years old, he told her point blank that he was ugly and could never be as good-looking as a White person. When she asked him why, he answered, "because they're just better than us at everything. We can never be as good as they are." Angry, heart-broken, and perplexed, Joanne pried a little deeper and found out that an older kid at school was routinely picking on her nephew and the basis of his taunting was the nephew's skin color. Deeply ashamed, Joanne's nephew later explained that this older kid kept telling him that he was so ugly and so dumb because he was so dark.

As we watch this young boy grow up in an environment that puts so much emphasis on one's looks, we become concerned for young Asian Americans. If we do not walk through our lives in our own skin with pride, if we do not teach younger generations to walk through their lives in their own skin with pride, then what kind of world are we crafting for them? No amount of skin lightening treatment or cosmetic surgery can erase the historical inequalities that force Asians and Asian Americans to feel inferior. Rather, by investing so deeply in such procedures, we tell them that the inequalities are justified. This is why it is imperative that we recognize, in the end, that the people who benefit from the lure of the beauty industry are not the clients who claim their self-esteem is so much higher because of treatments and surgeries. Instead, it is the business owners and the marketers who benefit from this industry, because they create the idea that Asians and Asian Americans are always just one surgery or one skin tone away from perfection.

NOTES

1. Let us not forget that the darker-skinned woman was also seen as hard working and virtuous—an assumption that has to do with the perception of her being an Asian immigrant who is trying to help her parents make ends meet. Consider how different this assumption would be if she were a Black woman.

Appendix 1: Colorism Interview Schedule

INTRODUCTORY AND BACKGROUND QUESTIONS

1. I'm interested in learning what people in the [Chinese, Filipino, Vietnamese, etc.] community think about the physical appearance of different members of that community. Specifically, I'm interested to find out whether people find certain kinds of appearance—skin color, hair, eyes, facial features, and such—more attractive than others. If possible, I'd like to find out why, and what implications such a preference may have.
2. Record time and place of interview. Get background information on the person:
   Age
   Gender
   Ethnicity
   Generation in this country (immigrants are first generation)
3. Ask the person to sign a permission form. Mark it with your initials and a number. Keep it separate from your notes and the transcript but mark those with your initials and the same number.

QUESTIONS ABOUT GENERAL COMMUNITY OPINION

4. Do you think people in your ethnic community prefer certain kinds of physical features over others? [possible prompts: skin color, nose shape, head shape, eye shape or color, height, weight]
5. Can you tell me a story about a situation you witnessed when someone showed that kind of preference?

possible follow-ups:

> What did other people think of this? Did they agree?
> What did you think of this?
> Do you know why they had that kind of preference?
> Can you tell me another story? (get as many as possible)

6. Do you think people in your ethnic community have stereotypes about people who have different complexions—light, medium, or dark skin? Can you tell me what those stereotypes might be?
7. Do you think people's opinions about this issue are different if they are immigrants versus those born or raised in the United States? Do you think that people who are more assimilated into American mainstream society see this issue differently from people who are less assimilated?
8. Do wealthy people in your ethnic community tend to have different features or skin tone or a different look than people who are less well off?
9. Do people in your ethnic community have different skin color or features preferences for women than for men? Do you think males or females care more about skin color? What makes you think that?
10. If people prefer lighter skin, do you think it is because they want to be White, or is it that they want to look like people who are more upper class, or is it something else?

QUESTIONS ABOUT WOMEN IN PHOTOGRAPHS

11. Show three photographs of women, arranged left to right, dark to light. Point at the woman in the middle first. Ask:

> What do you think of this woman?
> If you had to guess what her life was like, what would you guess?
> If I asked you to make up a story about something that happened to her, what would it be?

12. Repeat for the light woman.
13. Repeat for the dark woman.
14. a. For young women interviewees:

> Which of these women would you most like to be? Why?
> Which would be your second choice? Why?
> Why would you choose this one third?

b. For young men interviewees:

> Which of these women would you most like to date? Why?
> Which would be your second choice? Why?
> Why would you choose this one third?

c. For parental-generation interviewees:

> If you had a son, which of these women would you most like your son to marry? Why?
> Which would be your second choice? Why?
> Which would be your third choice? Why?

PERSONAL QUESTIONS

15. Can you recall any sayings or advice that you may have received from friends, family, or your community regarding skin color?
16. Who would your parents prefer to see you dating, marrying, and being friends with?

> Light, medium, or dark [Chinese, Filipino, Vietnamese, etc.]
> Other Asian (light, medium, or dark skinned)
> Non-Asian [White, Latino, Black, etc.]

17. Think back on your ex-boyfriends/ex-girlfriends (list them). Identify them by skin color. Is there a pattern of color, features, or ethnicity in them? Why do you think this is? What attracts you to certain sorts of people more than others?
18. Have you ever teased another person of your ethnic group because of their light, medium, or dark skin color or their features? Have you ever been teased by another member of your ethnic group on account of your skin color or features?
19. Have you ever punished or admonished another person of your ethnic group because of their light, medium, or dark skin color or their features? Have you ever been punished or admonished by another member of your ethnic group on account of your skin color or features?
20. How do you perceive the color of your own skin (light, medium, or dark)? Can you identify any personal experiences that may have influenced your perception?
21. If you could choose, would you be light, medium, or dark? Why did you choose that skin color? What might have influenced your decision?

22. If you could choose the color of your spouse, what color would that be? Why?
23. If you could choose the color of your baby, what color would that be? Why?
24. Have you ever used or considered using any cosmetic treatments for your skin color (e.g., tanning cream, bleaching treatments, color harmonizing agents, or consciously staying out of the sun)? What influenced you to use or consider using this treatment?
25. Do you have any other ancestry you know of or suspect besides [Chinese, Filipino, or Vietnamese, etc.]? If yes, is that ancestry something your family openly acknowledges? What does it mean to you and/or your family?

CONCLUDING QUESTIONS

26. Is there anything else you'd like to say? Thank you very much for your help with this project.
27. [after interview is over] Interviewer's estimate of interviewee's skin color:

    Dark   1   2   3   4   5   Light

Appendix 2: Interview Respondents' Demographic Data

#	Ethnicity	Gender	Generation	Age
1	Filipino	F	1	26
2	Filipino	F	2	29
3	Chinese/Cambodian	M	2	20
4	Chinese/Cambodian	F	2	20
5	Chinese/Cambodian	F	2	23
6	Chinese/Cambodian	M	1	33
7	Chinese/Cambodian	F	2	22
8	Chinese/Cambodian	F	2	23
9	Chinese/Cambodian	F	2	20
10	Chinese/Cambodian	F	1	36
11	Filipino	F	1	48
12	Filipino	F	2	21
13	Filipino	F	1	80
14	Filipino	M	1.5	22
15	Fil/Chin/Span/French	M	1.5	22
16	Filipino	M	1	20
17	Filipino	M	1	73
18	Filipino	F	1	40
19	Filipino	M	1	51
20	Vietnamese	M	1.5	22
21	Korean	F	1.5	21
22	Korean	F	2	21
23	Korean	M	2	18
24	Filipino	F	1	52
25	Filipino	F	1	58
26	Filipino	F	1	82
27	Filipino	F	1	30
28	Filipino	M	2	21
29	Filipino/Black	M	3	24
30	Cambodian	F	2	21

#	Ethnicity	Gender	Generation	Age
31	Cambodian	F	2	21
32	Chinese	F	2	18
33	Chinese	M	2	21
34	Vietnamese	F	2	21
35	Filipino	F	1	20
36	Cambodian/Chinese	F	2	20
37	Chinese	M	2	21
38	Chinese	M	2	21
39	Japanese	F	3	64
40	Japanese	F	1	54
41	Japanese	F	2	26
42	Japanese	F	2	23
43	Japanese	F	4	19
44	Japanese	M	4	19
45	Japanese	F	2	19
46	Japanese/Hispanic	F	2	19
47	Japanese	F	1	52
48	Indian/White	F	2	16
49	Filipino/Hispanic	F	3	19
50	Japanese	F	2	27
51	Japanese	M	1	50
52	Japanese	M	3	62
53	Chinese	M	2	21
54	Japanese	M	1	61
55	Japanese	M	4	31
56	Chinese	F	2	32
57	Chinese	F	2	22
58	Vietnamese/Chinese	M	2	21
59	Chinese	F	4	20
60	Chinese	F	2	19
61	Chinese	F	2	20
62	Fil/Chin/Ger/Irish	M	1	22
63	Filipino	F	3	22
64	Vietnamese	F	2	20
65	Cambodian	F	1	21
66	Taiwanese (Chinese)	M	1	22
67	Chinese	M	1	22
68	Filipino/Greek	F	2	21
69	Cambodian	F	1	20
70	Chinese/Vietnamese	M	2	21
71	Chinese	F	2	20
72	Korean	F	2	20
73	Taiwanese (Chinese)	M	1.5	21
74	Korean	F	2	21
75	Vietnamese	F	2	20
76	Chinese	M	4	19

#	Ethnicity	Gender	Generation	Age
77	Japanese	F	4	22
78	Filipino	F	1.5	26
79	Korean	M	2	24
80	Fil/Haw/Eng/Spn/Ger	M	3	19
81	Taiwanese (Chinese)	F	1	21
82	Filipino	M	2	20
83	Vietnamese	M	2	22
84	Cambodian/Chinese	F	1.5	19
85	Korean	F	1.5	21
86	Korean	F	2	19
87	South Asian	F	2	21
88	Korean	F	2	21
89	Filipino/White	F	2	23
90	Chinese	M	1	21
91	Filipino	F	1	64
92	Filipino	F	2	30
93	Filipino	F	1	63
94	Filipino	F	1.5	32
95	Filipino/Spanish	M	2	30
96	Filipino	M	1	55
97	Filipino	M	1	60
98	Filipino	M	1	64

Appendix 3: Cosmetic Surgery Interview Questions

FOR COSMETIC SURGEONS OR OTHER PEOPLE
WHO WORK IN PROVIDING PHYSICAL ALTERATIONS

Do you serve many Asian American patients? Mainly women or also
   men?

For what kinds of surgery do they consult you?

What seem to be the concerns behind Asian American patients coming
   to you?

   Eyelid alterations?
   Nose alterations?
   Bust enhancements?
   Liposuction?
   Other issues?

Are there particular features or issues that Asian American patients
   tend to be concerned about that are different from White or African
   American patients?

Do most people choose to undergo surgery after consulting you?

How does the rate compare to that for other populations?

Are there special problems from a surgical standpoint for procedures you
   use with Asian American patients?

What is the success rate? Is it different than for other procedures or
   populations?

Are your Asian American patients happy with the changes you have
   helped them make?

If they are not happy, what seems to be the pattern in the dissatisfaction?

FOR PEOPLE WHO HAVE HAD SURGICAL ALTERATIONS

What is the alteration you had?

What led you to choose that alteration?

    Did you feel badly about yourself before?

    Did people treat you badly about that feature before?

    Do you feel better about yourself since having the alteration?

    Do people treat you better regarding that feature since having the alteration?

What was the series of steps you went through?

    How did you decide to go to a physician?

    How did you choose a physician?

    Did he or she specialize in Asian American patients or procedures?

    Can you describe what took place on the day of the surgery?

    How did you feel?

    Can you describe what happened after the surgery and during your convalescence?

    How did you feel?

    Was your family supportive of the procedure?

    Before?

    During?

    After?

    Were your friends (especially boyfriends or girlfriends) supportive of the procedure?

    Before?

    During?

    After?

    How do you feel now about the procedure you went through?

    Better?

    Worse?

    About the same?

If you had it to do over, would you do this again?

    Would you counsel others to undergo a similar procedure?

Bibliography

Allen, Walter, Edward Telles, and Margaret Hunter. "Skin Color, Income and Education: A Comparison of African Americans and Mexican Americans." *National Journal of Sociology* 12, no. 1 (2000): 129–80.

Álvarez, Julia. "A White Woman of Color." In *Half + Half: Writers on Growing Up Biracial and Bicultural*, edited by Claudine Chiawei O'Hearn, 139–49. New York: Pantheon, 1998.

Arce, Carlos H., Edward Murguia, and W. Parker Frisbie. "Phenotype and Life Chances Among Chicanos." *Hispanic Journal of Behavioral Sciences* 9, no. 1 (1987): 19–32.

"Are Mulattoes Ruling the Race?" *Ebony* 9 (October 1954), 62–63.

Baker, Nancy C. *The Beauty Trap: Exploring Woman's Greatest Obsession.* New York: Franklin Watts, 1984.

Banner, Lois. *American Beauty.* New York: Knopf, 1983.

Barrera, Mario. *Race and Class in the Southwest.* Notre Dame, IN: University of Notre Dame Press, 1982.

Berlin, Ira. *Slaves Without Masters: The Free Negro in the Antebellum South.* New York: Knopf, 1974.

Bond, Selena, and Thomas Cash. "Black Beauty: Skin Color and Body Images among African American College Women." *Journal of Applied Social Psychology* 22 (1992): 874–88.

Bonner, Lonnice. *Good Hair.* New York: Crown, 1991.

Bordo, Susan. *Unbearable Weight: Feminism, Western Culture, and the Body.* Berkeley: University of California Press, 2003.

Brand, Peg Zeglin, ed. *Beauty Matters.* Bloomington: Indiana University Press, 2000.

Brooks, James F., ed. *Confounding the Color Line: The Indian-Black Experience in North America.* Lincoln: University of Nebraska Press, 2002.

Byrd, Ayana, and Lori Tharps. *Hair Story: Untangling the Roots of Black Hair in America.* New York: St. Martin's, 2001.

Cash, Thomas, and Nancy C. Duncan. "Physical Attractiveness Stereotyping Among Black American College Students." *Journal of Social Psychology* 122 (1984): 71–77.

Chambers, John W., Jr., Tangela Clark, Leatha Dantzler, and Joseph A. Baldwin. "Perceived Attractiveness, Facial Features, and African Self-Consciousness." *Journal of Black Psychology* 20, no. 3 (1994): 305–24.

Chapkis, Wendy. *Beauty Secrets: Women and the Politics of Appearance.* Boston: South End Press, 1986.

Coard, Stephanie Irby, Alfiee M. Breland, and Patricia Raskin. "Perceptions of and Preferences for Skin Color, Black Racial Identity and Self-Esteem among African Americans." *Journal of Applied Social Psychology* 31 (2001): 2256–75.

Codina, G. Edward, and Frank F. Montalvo. "Chicano Phenotype and Depression." *Hispanic Journal of Behavioral Sciences* 16, no. 3 (1994): 296–306.

Corderi, Victoria. "Plastic Surgery Tourism? Dangers of Going Under the Knife Cheap." *Dateline NBC*, 2005.

Cox, Oliver C. *Caste, Class, and Race.* 1948. Reprint, New York: Monthly Review Press, 1970.

Daniel, G. Reginald. "Passers and Pluralists: Subverting the Racial Divide." In *Racially Mixed People in America*, edited by Maria P. P. Root, 91–107. Newbury Park, CA: Sage, 1992.

———. "Either Black or White: Race, Modernity, and the Law of the Excluded Middle." In *Racial Thinking in the United States*, edited by Paul Spickard and G. Reginald Daniel, 21–59. Notre Dame, IN: University of Notre Dame Press, 2004.

Davis, Allison, Burleigh B. Gardner, and Mary R. Gardner. *Deep South: A Social Anthropological Study of Caste and Class*, abridged ed. Chicago: University of Chicago Press, 1965.

Davis, F. James. *Who Is Black? One Nation's Definition.* University Park: Pennsylvania State University Press, 1991.

Davis, Kathy. "A 'Dubious Equality': Men, Women and Cosmetic Surgery," *Body and Society* 8, no. 1 (2002).

———. *Reshaping the Female Body.* New York: Routledge, 1995.

Dikötter, Frank, ed. *The Construction of Racial Identities in China and Japan.* Stanford, CA: Stanford University Press, 1997.

Dollard, John. *Caste and Class in a Southern Town*, 3rd ed. Garden City, N.Y.: Doubleday, 1957.

Dotson, Edisol W. *Behold the Man: The Hype and Selling of Male Beauty in Media and Culture.* New York: Haworth Press, 1999.

Drake, St. Clair, and Horace Cayton. *Black Metropolis.* New York: Harcourt, Brace, 1945.

Du Bois, W. E. Burghardt. *Dusk of Dawn: An Essay Toward an Autobiography of a Race Concept.* 1940. Reprint, New Brunswick, N.J.: Transaction, 1984.

Edwards, G. Franklin. *The Negro Professional Class.* Glencoe, IL: Free Press, 1959.

Edwards, Ozzie L. "Skin Color as a Variable in Racial Attitudes of Black Urbanites." *Journal of Black Studies* 3, no. 4 (1972): 473–83.

Fanon, Frantz. *Black Skin, White Masks.* New York: Grove, 1967.

Ferguson, Marjorie. *Forever Feminine: Women's Magazines and the Cult of Femininity.* Brookfield, U.K.: Gower, 1985.

Fitzpatrick, Joseph P. "The Problem of Color." In *Puerto Rican Americans*, 101–14. Englewood Cliffs, N.J.: Prentice-Hall, 1971.

Frazier, E. Franklin. *Black Bourgeoisie: The Rise of a New Middle Class.* New York: Free Press, 1957.

———. *The Negro Family in the United States.* 1939. Reprint, Notre Dame, IN: University of Notre Dame Press, 2001.

Freedman, Rita. *Beauty Bound.* Lexington, Mass.: Lexington Books, 1986.

Freeman, Howard E., J. Michael Ross, David Armor, and Thomas F. Pettigrew. "Color Gradation and Attitudes Among Middle-Income Negroes." *American Sociological Review* 31, no. 3 (1966): 365–74.

Gatewood, Willard B. *Aristocrats of Color: The Black Elite, 1880–1920.* Bloomington: Indiana University Press, 1990.

———. "Skin Color." In *Encyclopedia of Afro-American Culture and History*, edited by Jack Salzman, David Lionel Smith, and Cornel West, 2444–49. New York: Macmillan, 1996.

Genocchio, Benjamin. "For Japanese Girls, Black Is Beautiful." *New York Times* (August 4, 2004).

Gergen, Kenneth J. "The Significance of Skin Color in Human Relations." *Daedalus* 96 (1967): 390–406.

Gibson, Aliona L. *Nappy: Growing Up Black and Female in America.* New York: Harlem River Press, 1995.

Gillem, Angela R., and Cathy A. Thompson, eds. *Biracial Women in Therapy.* New York: Haworth Press, 2004.

Gilman, Sandra L. *Creating Beauty to Cure the Soul: Race and Psychology in the Shaping of Aesthetic Surgery.* Durham, N.C.: Duke University Press, 1998.

Gimlin, Debra L. *Body Work: Beauty and Self-Image in American Culture.* Berkeley: University of California Press, 2002.

Graham, Lawrence. *Our Kind of People: Inside America's Black Upper Class.* New York: Harper Collins, 1999.

Green, Kim. "The Pain of Living the Lye." *Essence* (June 1993), 38.

Hackley, Azalia. *The Colored Girl Beautiful.* Kansas City: Burton, 1916.

Haiken, Elizabeth. *Venus Envy. The History of Cosmetic Surgery.* Baltimore: Johns Hopkins University Press, 1997.

Hale, Grace. *Making Whiteness: The Culture of Segregation in the South, 1890–1940.* New York: Random House, 1998.

Hall, Ronald E. "The Bleaching Syndrome: African Americans' Response to Cultural Domination Vis-à-Vis Skin Color." *Journal of Black Studies* 26, no. 2 (1995): 172–84.

———. "The 'Bleaching Syndrome': Implications of Light Skin for Hispanic American Assimilation." *Hispanic Journal of Behavioral Sciences* 16, no. 3 (1994): 307–14.

———. "Eurogamy Among Asian-Americans: A Note on Western Assimilation." *Social Science Journal* 34, no. 3 (1997), 403–08.

Harris, Cheryl, "Whiteness as Property." *Harvard Law Review*, 106 (1993).

Harris, Robert L., Jr. "Charleston's Free Afro-American Elite." *South Carolina Historical Magazine* 82, no. 4 (1981), 289–310.

Harvey, Aminifu R. "The Issue of Skin Color in Psychotherapy with African Americans." *Families in Society* 76, no. 1 (1995): 3–10.

Herring, Cedric. "Skin Deep: Race and Complexion in the 'Color Blind' Era." In *Skin/Deep: How Race and Complexion Matter in the "Color Blind" Era*, edited by Cedric Herring, Verna M. Keith, and Hayward Derrick Horton, 1–21. Urbana: University of Illinois Press, 2004.

Herring, Cedric, Verna M. Keith, and Hayward Derrick Horton, eds. *Skin/Deep: How Race and Complexion Matter in the "Color Blind" Era*. Urbana: University of Illinois Press, 2004.

Hill, Mark E. "Color Differences in the Socioeconomic Status of African American Men." *Social Forces* 78, no. 4 (2000): 1437–60.

———. "Skin Color and the Perception of Attractiveness Among African Americans: Does Gender Make a Difference?" *Social Psychology Quarterly* 65 (2002), 77–91.

Hill-Collins, Patricia. *Black Feminist Thought*. New York: Routledge, 2000.

Hodes, Martha. *White Women, Black Men: Illicit Sex in the 19th-Century South*. New Haven, CT: Yale University Press, 1997.

Holtzman, Jo. "Color Caste Changes among Black College Students." *Journal of Black Studies* 4, no. 1 (1973): 92–101.

hooks, bell. *Black Looks: Race and Representation*. Boston: South End Press, 1992.

Hopkins, Tracy E. "The Darker the Berry." In *Testimony*, edited by Natasha Tarpley, 231–35. Boston: Beacon, 1995.

Horowitz, Donald L. "Color Differentiation in the American Systems of Slavery." *Journal of Interdisciplinary History* 3, no. 3 (1973): 509–41.

Hughes, Michael, and Bradley Hertel. "The Significance of Color Remains: A Study of Life Chances, Mate Selection, and Ethnic Consciousness Among Black Americans." *Social Forces* 68 (1990): 1105–20.

Hunter, Margaret. "Colorstruck: Skin Color Stratification in the Lives of African American Women." *Sociological Inquiry* 68, no. 4 (1998): 517–35.

———. "'If You're Light You're Alright': Light Skin Color as Social Capital for Women of Color." *Gender and Society* 16, no. 2 (2002): 175–93.

———. *Race, Gender, and the Politics of Skin Tone*. New York: Routledge, 2005.

———. "Light, Bright, and Almost White: The Advantages and Disadvantages of Light Skin." In *Skin/Deep: How Race and Complexion Matter in the "Color Blind" Era*, edited by Cedric Herring, Verna M. Keith, and Hayward Derrick Horton, 22–44. Urbana: University of Illinois Press, 2004.

———. "The *Lighter* the Berry? Race, Color, and Gender in the Lives of African American and Mexican American Women." Ph.D. diss., UCLA, 1999.

Johnson, Charles S. *Growing Up in the Black Belt: Negro Youth in the Rural South*. 1941. Reprint, New York: Schocken, 1970.

Jones, Lisa. *Bulletproof Diva: Tales of Race, Sex, and Hair*. New York: Doubleday, 1994.

Jordan, Winthrop D. "American Chiaroscuro: The Status and Definition of Mulattoes in the British Colonies." *William and Mary Quarterly* 3rd ser., 19 (1962): 183–200.

———. "The 'One-Drop' Racial 'Rule' in the United States." Unpublished manuscript courtesy of the author.

———. *The White Man's Burden: Historical Origins of Racism in the United States*. New York: Oxford, 1974.

———. *White Over Black: American Attitudes Toward the Negro, 1550–1812*. Chapel Hill: University of North Carolina Press, 1968.

Kaw, Eugenia. "Medicalization of Racial Features: Asian American Women and Cosmetic Surgery," *Medical Anthropology Quarterly* 7, no. 1 (1993).

Keith, Verna M., and Cedric Herring. "Skin Tone Stratification in the Black Community." *American Journal of Sociology* 97, no. 3 (1991): 760–78.

Kimura, Margaret. *Asian Beauty*. New York: Harper Collins, 2001.

King-O'Riain, Rebecca Chiyoko. *Pure Beauty: Judging Race in Japanese American Beauty Pageants*. Minneapolis: University of Minnesota Press, 2006.

Lake, Obiagele. *Blue Veins and Kinky Hair: Naming and Color Consciousness in African America*. Westport, CT: Praeger, 2003.

Lakoff, Robin, and Racquel Scherr. *Face Value: The Politics of Beauty*. Boston: Routledge, 1984.

Landry, Bart. *The New Black Middle Class*. Berkeley: University of California Press, 1987.

Lipsitz, George. *The Possessive Investment in Whiteness: How White People Profit from Identity Politics*. Philadelphia: Temple University Press, 1998.

Little, Benilde. *Good Hair*. New York: Simon and Schuster, 1996.

Longshore, Douglas. "Color Connotations and Racial Attitudes." *Journal of Black Studies* 10, no. 2 (1979), 183–97.

Lutz, Catherine, and Jane L. Collins. *Reading National Geographic*. Chicago: University of Chicago Press, 1993.

Martinez, George. "Mexican Americans and Whiteness." In *Critical White Studies*, edited by Richard Delgado and Jean Stefancic. Philadelphia: Temple University Press, 1997.

Mississippi Masala. VHS. Directed by Mira Nair. Culver City, CA: SCS Films, Columbia TriStar Home Video, 1992.

Moore, Jacqueline M. *Leading the Race: The Transformation of the Black Elite in the Nation's Capital, 1880–1920*. Charlottesville: University of Virginia Press, 1999.

Murguia, Edward, and Edward E. Telles. "Phenotype and Schooling among Mexican Americans." *Sociology of Education* 69 (1996): 276–89.

Myrdal, Gunnar. *An American Dilemma: The Negro Problem and Modern Democracy*, 2 vols. New York: Harper and Row, 1944.

Naipaul, V. S. *Half a Life*. New York: Knopf, 2001.

Neal, Angela. "The Influence of Skin Color and Facial Features on Perceptions of Black Female Physical Attractiveness." Ph.D. diss., DePaul University, 1988.

Neal, Angela M., and Midge L. Wilson. "The Role of Skin Color and Features in the Black Community: Implications for Women and Therapy." *Clinical Psychology Review* 9 (1989): 323–33.

"Negro Blue Bloods." *Ebony*, 10 (September 1955), 55.

Okazawa-Rey, Margo, Tracey Robinson, and Janie Victoria Ward. "Black Women and the Politics of Skin Color and Hair." *Women's Studies Quarterly* 14, nos. 1–2 (1986): 13–14.

———. "Black Women and the Politics of Skin Color and Hair." *Women and Therapy* 6 (1987): 89–102.

Omi, Michael, and Howard Winant. *Racial Formation from the 1960s to the 1990s.* New York: Routledge, 1994.

Park, Lisa. "A Letter to My Sister." In *Making More Waves: New Writing by Asian American Women,* edited by Elaine Kim, et al. Boston: Beacon, 1997.

Parrish, Charles. "The Significance of Skin Color in the Negro Community." Ph.D. diss., University of Chicago, 1944.

Patillo-McCoy, Mary. *Black Picket Fences: Privilege and Peril among the Black Middle Class.* Chicago: University of Chicago Press, 1999.

Peiss, Kathy. *Hope in a Jar: The Making of America's Beauty Culture.* New York: Metropolitan Books, 1998.

Porter, Cornelia P. "Social Reasons for Skin Tone Preferences of Black School-Aged Children." *American Journal of Orthopsychiatry* 61 (1991): 149–54.

Powdermaker, Hortense. *After Freedom: A Cultural Study in the Deep South.* 1939. Reprint, Madison: University of Wisconsin Press, 1993.

Ransford, H. Edward. "Skin Color, Life Chances, and Anti-White Attitudes." *Social Problems* 18 (1970): 164–79.

Relethford, John H., Michael P. Stern, Sharon P. Gaskill, and Helen P. Hazuda. "Social Class, Admixture, and Skin Color Variation in Mexican Americans and Anglo Americans Living in San Antonio, Texas." *American Journal of Physical Anthropology* 61 (1983): 97–102.

Reuter, Edward Byron. *The Mulatto in the United States.* 1918. Reprint, New York: Negro Universities Press, 1969.

Robbins, Faye Wellborn. "A World-within-a-World: Black Nashville, 1880–1915." PhD diss., University of Arkansas, Little Rock, 1980.

Rodríguez, Clara E. *Changing Race: Latinos, the Census, and the History of Ethnicity in the United States.* New York: NYU Press, 2000.

———. *Puerto Ricans: Born in the USA.* Boulder, CO: Westview, 1991.

Rooks, Noliwe. *Hair Raising: Beauty, Culture, and African American Women.* New Brunswick, N.J.: Rutgers University Press, 1996.

Root, Deborah. *Cannibal Culture: Art, Appropriation, and the Commodification of Difference.* Boulder, CO: Westview, 1998.

Ross, Louie E. "Mate Selection Preferences Among African-American College Students." *Journal of Black Studies* 27, no. 4 (1997): 554–69.

Russell, Kathy, Midge Wilson, and Ronald Hall. *The Color Complex: The Politics of Skin Color Among African Americans.* New York: Harcourt Brace Jovanovich, 1992.

Ruiz, Vicki. *From Out of the Shadows: Mexican Women in Twentieth-Century America.* New York: Oxford, 1998.

Sahay, Sarita, and Niva Piran. "Skin Color Preferences and Body Satisfaction among South Asian-Canadian and European-Canadian Female University Students." *Journal of Social Psychology* 137, no. 2 (1997): 167–71.

Seltzer, Richard, and Robert C. Smith. "Color Differences in the Afro-American Community and the Differences They Make." *Journal of Black Studies* 21, no. 3 (1991): 279–86.

Small, Stephen. "Mustefinos Are White by Law: Whites and People of Mixed Racial Origins in Historical and Comparative Perspective." In *Racial Thinking in the United States*, edited by Paul Spickard and G. Reginald Daniel, 60–79. Notre Dame, IN: University of Notre Dame Press, 2004.

Spickard, Paul. *Mixed Blood: Intermarriage and Ethnic Identity in Twentieth-Century America*. Madison: University of Wisconsin Press, 1989.

———. "The Power of Blackness: Mixed-Race Leaders and the Monoracial Ideal." In *Racial Thinking in the United States*, edited by Paul Spickard and G. Reginald Daniel, 103–23. Notre Dame, IN: University of Notre Dame Press, 2004.

Strutton, David, and James R. Lumplein. "Stereotypes of Black In-Group Attractiveness in Advertising." *Psychological Reports* 73 (1993): 507–11.

Takaki, Ronald. *Iron Cages: Race and Culture in Nineteenth-Century America.* New York: Knopf, 1979.

Telles, Edward E., and Edward Murguia. "Phenotypic Discrimination and Income Differences among Mexican Americans." *Social Science Quarterly* 71, no. 4 (1990): 682–96.

Thompson, Maxine S., and Verna M. Keith. "The Blacker the Berry: Gender, Skin Tone, Self-Esteem and Self-Efficacy." *Gender and Society* 15, no. 3 (2001): 336–57.

Thurman, Wallace. *The Blacker the Berry.* 1929; London: X Press, 1994.

Tilley, Virginia Q. "*Mestizaje* and the 'Ethnicization' of Race in Latin America." In *Race and Nation: Ethnic Systems in the Modern World*, edited by Paul Spickard, 51–66. New York: Routledge, 2005.

Toplin, Robert Brent. "Between Black and White: Attitudes Toward Southern Mulattoes, 1830–1861." *Journal of Southern History* 45, no. 2 (1979): 185–200.

Tuan, Mia. *Forever Foreigners or Honorary Whites? The Asian Ethnic Experience Today.* New Brunswick, N.J.: Rutgers University Press, 1998.

Udry, J. Richard. "The Importance of Being Beautiful: A Re-examination and Racial Comparison." *American Journal of Sociology* 83, no. 1 (1977), 154–60.

Udry, J. Richard, Karl E. Bauman, and Charles Chase. "Skin Color, Status, and Mate Selection." *American Journal of Sociology* 76, no. 1 (1971), 722–33.

Vásquez, Luis A., Enedina García-Vásquez, Sheri A. Bauman, and Arturo S. Sierra. "Skin Culture, Acculturation, and Community Interest Among Mexican American Students." *Hispanic Journal of Behavioral Sciences* 19, no. 3 (1997): 377–86.

Wade, T. Joel. "The Relationship Between Skin Color and Self-Perceived Global, Physical and Sexual Attractiveness, and Self-esteem for African-Americans." *Journal of Black Psychology* 22, no. 3 (1996): 358–73.

Wagatsuma, Hiroshi. "The Social Perception of Skin Color in Japan." *Daedalus* 96, no. 2 (1967): 407–43.

Warner, W. Lloyd, Buford H. Junker, and Walter A. Adams. *Color and Human Nature: Negro Personality Development in a Northern City.* 1941. Reprint, New York: Harper, 1969.

Washington, Jesse. "A Lighter Shade of Black." *Essence* (January 1995), 40.

West, Dorothy. *The Wedding*. New York: Doubleday, 1995.

White, Walter. *Flight*. 1926. Reprint, Baton Rouge: Louisiana State University Press, 1998.

Williamson, Joel. *New People: Miscegenation and Mulattoes in the United States.* New York: Macmillan, 1980.

Wolf, Naomi. *The Beauty Myth*. New York: Doubleday, 1991.

Index

About the Authors

THE AUTHORS

Joanne L. Rondilla is a doctoral candidate in Ethnic Studies at the University of California, Berkeley. She is the coeditor, with Paul Spickard and Debbie Hippolite Wright, of *Pacific Diaspora: Island Peoples in the United States and Across the Pacific* (2002). Born and raised in Guam, Joanne is the youngest child of Sonia and Fernando Rondilla. She is also a freelance skincare specialist, *krav maga* enthusiast, and proud auntie.

Paul Spickard teaches history and Asian American studies at the University of California, Santa Barbara. He is the author or editor of more than a dozen books, including *Racial Thinking in the United States* (2004) and *Race and Nation: Ethnic Systems in the Modern World* (2005). His current project is *Almost All Aliens: Immigration, Race, and Colonialism in American History and Identity* (to be published in 2007).

CONTRIBUTING RESEARCHERS AND WRITERS

Lilynda Agvateesiri earned her B. A. in Communication at the University of California, Santa Barbara. She currently lives in the San Francisco Bay Area and works in corporate business development. She enjoys traveling, gourmet cooking, strength training, and wine tasting in her spare time.

Monica Chum studied History and Asian American Studies at the University of California, Santa Barbara. She is currently specializing in finance and investment in Southern California.

Sara Cruz graduated from the University of California, Santa Barbara, with a B. A. in sociology in 2004. Currently living in Valencia after a sojourn in Ireland, she is pursuing a career in university career services.

Luz Devadason graduated from the University of California, Santa Barbara, and is currently pursuing a career in the arts.

Holly Hoegi did her undergraduate work at the University of California, Santa Barbara, in Asian American Studies. She earned a law degree from Southwestern School of Law and is an attorney in Los Angeles.

After completing a B. A. at the University of California, Santa Barbara, and a sojourn in Australia, **Karen Jackson** works in advertising in San Francisco.

Lynn Kawabe was an undergraduate at the University of California, Santa Barbara. She is currently completing a master's degree in marriage and family therapy and plans to pursue a doctorate in clinical psychology.

Marybeth Liu is a freelance writer and photographer currently living and working in Colorado.

Christie Trieu has a B. A. in Asian American Studies and a minor in Women's Studies from the University of California, Santa Barbara. She is currently working on a multiple-subjects teaching credential with an emphasis on Asian language instruction.

Charmaine Tuason graduated from the University of California, Santa Barbara, with a B. A. in Asian American Studies. A perpetual student, Charmaine is currently pursuing studies in Music. She lives in California's beautiful central coast.

Mey Year completed a B. A. at the University of California, Santa Barbara and is currently conducting research in the pharmaceutical industry.